Can **Two** Walk **Together?**

Can **Two** Walk **Together?**

Encouragement for
Spiritually Unbalanced Marriages

Sabrina D. Black

MOODY PRESS
CHICAGO

Scripture quotations marked KJV are taken from the King James Version.

Scripture quotations marked NIV are taken from the *Holy Bible, New International Version.*® NIV.® Copyright © 1973, 1978, 1984 by International Bible Society. Used by permission of Zondervan Publishing House. All rights reserved.

Scripture quotations marked NASB are taken from the *New American Standard* Bible,® Copyright © The Lockman Foundation 1960, 1962, 1963, 1968, 1971, 1972, 1973, 1975, 1977, 1995. Used by permission.

Scripture quotations marked TLB are taken from *The Living Bible* copyright © 1971. Used by permission of Tyndale House Publishers, Inc., Wheaton, Illinois 60189. All rights reserved.

Scripture quotations marked AMPLIFIED are taken from the *Amplified Bible, Old Testament,* Copyright © 1965, 1987 by The Zondervan Corporation. *The Amplified Bible,* New Testament, copyright © 1954, 1958, 1987 by The Lockman Foundation. Used by permission.

Library of Congress Cataloging-in-Publication Data

Black, Sabrina D.
   Can two walk together? / by Sabrina D. Black
      p. cm.
   ISBN 0-8024-1771-X
      1. Spouses—Religious life. 2. Non-church affiliated people—Family
         relationships.
      2. Marriage—Religious aspects—Christianity. I. Title

   BV4596.M3 .B57 2002
   248.8'44—dc21

                                                        2002024432

3 5 7 9 10 8 6 4 2
Printed in the United States of America

This book is dedicated to my loving and supportive husband,
Warren José Black.
Thank you for sharing your life with me
and for allowing me to share our lives with others.
God has used every day
and every situation in our lives
to draw me closer to Him.
This book would not have been possible without you.

Contents

Forewords

Several years ago I spoke to a large conference of Christian counselors and tried to paint a visionary perspective on what the future of counseling could be like. The audience was polite and attentive but counselors are not always inclined to be thinking about future or visionary ideas. About two hours after my talk I ran into Sabrina Black in the lobby of the conference hotel. "I have a present for you," she exclaimed enthusiastically, and then presented me with a tee shirt with the words "Don't let the vision vanish." The shirts had been prepared for a conference where she was speaking in Africa and she had an extra that she gave me.

All through a sometimes difficult marriage, Sabrina never let the vision of a better marriage vanish. Her book applies this message to readers who may wonder if things will ever get better. With honesty, examples from her own experience, abundant Scripture, a wealth of practical guidance, and a captivating writing style, Sabrina deals with the challenge of living in a marriage where one person is a follower of Jesus and the other is not.

Every reader will find something of value in this book, including the sweet spirit of a writer who freely points to her own mistakes and failures in trying to make her "unequally yoked" marriage work. Without criticism or a hint of anger, she consistently affirms her husband even as she honestly describes the impact of his attitudes, criticisms and non-Christian friends who so often created tensions for his Christian wife.

If you hope for a better marriage, and the ultimate salvation of your spouse, Sabrina Black's book will give you a wealth of practical help and encouragement. Her message to you is the message on that tee shirt. When it comes to thinking about a better marriage, "Don't let the vision vanish."

I am glad to recommend this book enthusiastically.

Dr. Gary R. Collins

Sabrina Black speaks a language we can all understand. She writes with the insight of a counselor and the heart of a minister. Her new book, *Can Two Walk Together?* tackles the tough questions regarding unequally yoked marriages. She leaves no stone unturned as she examines biblical teaching, psychological assessment, and her own personal experience.

Your mind will be stretched and your heart will be moved as you read through the pages of this powerful new book. It is the most thorough treatment of this issue that I have ever seen. It is ideal for pastors, counselors, and Christian workers who face these questions every single day. I highly recommend it for both individual and group study. It is a wonderful book filled with hope, help, and healing.

The Bible study section alone is worth the price of the book. Every verse of Scripture that is pertinent to this issue is analyzed and examined. You can't miss what God has to say about this matter. It is all laid out in black and white. Read it, enjoy it, and do it. Your life will be blessed and your marriage will be enriched.

Ed Hindson, PhD.
Assistant Chancellor
Liberty University
Lynchburg, Virginia

Acknowledgments

I gratefully acknowledge:

My Lord and Savior, the almighty God: for salvation and the abundant life; for enlarging my territory and allowing me to make a local and global impact.

My husband, Warren José Black: who truly taught me about the love of God, the grace of God, and the mercy of God; for encouraging me (in his own way) in every endeavor.

My parents, Clyde and Adell Dickinson: for modeling a godly marriage; my father for loving my mother as Christ loved the church and giving himself for her; my mother who modeled godliness through discipline and demonstrated submission to my father with reverence and joy.

My administrative assistant, Ramona Tillman: for her labor of love as she typed, edited, and researched information for this book and my numerous other projects; for being a young woman whose heart's desire is to please God and for being open enough to share her life struggles.

My initial editor, Denise Gates: for embracing this project with love and spending many hours in prayer and fasting; for her patience as God worked in both of us, "iron sharpening iron."

My accountability group: LaVern Harlin (14 years), Latitia Watkins (30 years), Hivenna Crockett (4 years).

My pastors: Rev. Haman Cross Jr. and Rev. Gregory Alexander—who provided counsel and encouragement along the way.

My prayer support team: Harriet Smith (coordinator), Cynthia Chestnut, Charmane Coleman, Hivenna Crockett, Adell Dickinson, Rebecca Doll, LaVern Harlin, Debbie Haskins, Laurie Henry, Brenda Jenkins, Pam Hudson, Debby Mitchell, Lori Morton, Debra Nixon, Ramona B. Tillman, Rebecca Trivilino, Doshia Wallace, Latitia Watkins.

The preview team: Valda Atkinson, Renee Carter, Charmane Coleman, Adell Dickinson, Rebecca Doll, Karen Harlin, Debbie Haskins, Pam Hudson, Debra Nixon, Kaye Pottinger, Harriet Smith, Doshia Wallace.

Earlene Lindsay Richardson: for providing the first public platform to tell my story and helping to establish me as a women's conference speaker.

Renee Carter: for inviting me to Rosedale where I came to know and develop an intimate relationship with Jesus Christ; for discipling me for three years as I learned to love and live the Word of God.

Those who encouraged me in the early years: Valerie Myers (initial transcriptions), Monica Johnson (American Christian Writers group leader), Doriece Denson (prayer partner), Dorris Reese (Speak Up with Confidence), Linda White (faithful friend and prayer partner).

The writers who have gone before and have helped to show me the way.

With much gratitude and appreciation!

Sabrina

Introduction

Whatever your reason is for reading this—whether it is to find help for your personal situation, for someone else, or because of a ministry that the Lord is ready to develop in your life—I am glad you have started this journey.

You are not holding this book by accident. There is something within these pages that you need to read—if not for yourself, then because the Lord knows that you will meet someone else who needs to hear the message you receive. So again, it is not by accident that you are reading this; I believe it is by divine appointment.

If you are unequally yoked (spiritually unbalanced), you are not alone. Just think for a moment. You probably know many people who are in unequally yoked relationships in your family, among your friends, in your church, at work, and in your community. However, my experience has been that people don't know what to say, and they don't know what to do. They want to help, but they don't know how. *Can*

Two Walk Together? provides that much-needed encouragement for those who are unequally yoked.

When you are in an unequally yoked relationship, you are definitely seeking and searching for those who know how to minister to you. In most churches, different groups come together for fellowship and ministry. You'll find the children's ministry, the youth ministry, the singles' ministry, and the couples' ministry. There is even a ministry for those who are widowed and divorced. However, there is rarely a ministry to equip, support, and encourage people who are unequally yoked. And the congregation is filled with people who are in this situation.

People in unbalanced or unequally yoked relationships are part of a special population that is dear to my heart. You see, for many years I was part of this population. I am indeed a wounded healer. The things in my marriage that the Lord has allowed me to live through (as difficult as they seemed) have given me great insight and wisdom.

Our God comforts us in all our troubles so that we can comfort others with the comfort that we have received from Him. "Blessed be God, even the Father of our Lord Jesus Christ, the Father of mercies, and the God of all comfort; Who comforteth us in all our tribulation, that we may be able to comfort them which are in any trouble, by the comfort wherewith we ourselves are comforted of God" (2 Corinthians 1:3–4 KJV). The Lord has helped me to process my own personal pain, and He has given me an opportunity to help others.

God has been so good to me, and He has blessed me in abundance. I have been married for over fifteen years. I praise God that He has sustained us. We have moved from survival to revival; now we are thriving. However, it has not always been easy.

I have my husband's permission to share these things. Whenever I discuss our marriage, he is very much aware of what I say. I have great admiration and respect for my husband because I truly love him. It was a result of the things that I learned through dealing with him that forced me to my knees and drew me closer to God. It is amazing how God uses our nonbelieving spouses! I often wonder what my life would have been like had we not been unequally yoked. I know that spiritually I have grown by leaps and bounds as a result of laboring in prayer for him, our marriage, and for myself.

When José and I married, neither one of us knew the Lord. I had heard of God. I knew that God did great things, but I did not have a personal relationship with Him. When I accepted Christ during our second year of marriage, it was a culture shock for my husband. Our entire world changed.

At first, I could not understand why José was missing it. How could he fail to share my excitement about the Lord? Why didn't he want to join me in the faith? In Scripture, the apostle Paul writes, "Brethren, my heart's desire and prayer to God for Israel is, that they might be saved" (Romans 10:1 KJV). That was my heart's desire—that my husband would be saved.

As time passed, God reminded me of some obvious truths: He is the One who moves the hearts of men. Even with the best intentions, I could not make my husband seek after God. I could not make him come to church. I could beg, plead, cry, and do many things in the flesh (without God's direction), but only God could change his heart.

What I share in this book is how God has blessed me, challenged me, and caused me to grow in an unbalanced marital relationship. I also share how it has made a difference in the life of my husband, who in the fourteenth year of our marriage gave his heart to the Lord. I have learned that the power of God can be available in unequally yoked relationships. (Yes, the power of God can be active and available even in unequally yoked relationships!)

I encourage you to avoid the temptation to breeze through the information contained in these chapters. Instead, stop frequently and take the time to think about your own marital situation. Use the spaces in the companion Bible Study Workbook to record notes as you reflect on the concepts and answer the questions that correspond to the content of each chapter.

When you finish a chapter, you may wish to pray. Ask God for specific answers, wisdom, and revelation. For example: "How does this apply to my life?" "What part of my relationship is revealed in what is written?" "What kind of practical changes should I make when I put this book down?"

It is my sincere desire that the truth of God's Word and the power of God will become part of your life experience and that you will become empowered to minister His truth to others.

Let's pray together before you begin.

> *Dear Lord, We thank You for Your goodness and Your mercy. By faith, we know it is Your power active and available in our lives and in our marriages that will sustain us. Lord, please help us to just glance at our current situation and to gaze upon You. For we know that our strength and power comes from You.*
>
> *Father, I thank You for my sisters (and brothers) who are reading this book. I pray that through the experiences, ideas, and biblical principles shared in these pages they will gain wisdom and insight to equip and empower them, in every situation, to live a life that is pleasing to You.*
>
> *May Your presence and Your peace be tangible as You prepare their hearts to receive the message that You have sent—a message that is just for them. In Jesus' name. Amen.*

CHAPTER ONE

The Power
of God—Active
and Available

If you've ever tried to do a difficult thing in your own strength, you know how quickly you become tired. Just surviving from day to day sometimes seems like a miracle. God's power is always available; but if we don't avail ourselves of it, what difference does it make for us? It is like having money in the bank and living like you are poor, when all you have to do is make a withdrawal.

Scripture says that God gives strength and power to His people (Psalm 68:35; Matthew 9:8; 2 Timothy 1:7). There is power in the name of the Lord, there is power in the blood, there is power in God's Word, and there is power in the testimony of the saints. We must learn to activate God's power in our lives, in our everyday situations, and in our marriages. All we have to do is fall down on our knees and pray; all we have to do is ask and receive, and trust and obey.

I guess you're thinking, "That's easy for you to say, but how can I do this?" I promise you, my friend, it is not easy for me because I am weak. However, you must remember, I am not doing this thing and neither will you. God in us transforms our marriages. The strength is in Him!

BE STRONG IN THE LORD

Ephesians 6:10 is a verse that has really ministered to me. You can encourage others with this same verse. Following are five different translations of this verse. As you read each, stop and think about what the verse says to you before going on to read the next one.

Finally, my brethren, be strong in the Lord, and in the power of his might. (KJV)

Finally, be strong in the Lord and in the strength of His might. (NASB)

Finally, be strong in the Lord and in his mighty power. (NIV)

Last of all I want to remind you that your strength must come from the Lord's mighty power within you. (TLB)

In conclusion, be strong in the Lord—be empowered through your union with Him; draw your strength from Him—that strength which His [boundless] might provides. (AMPLIFIED)

In *Strong's Exhaustive Concordance of the Bible,* the word "finally" means furthermore; from now on; henceforth; moreover. Therefore, the Word of God says: No matter what your situation is—whatever you are facing—from henceforth, be strong in the Lord. You may be feeling weak, tired, or fed up. You may be wondering what you're going to do, and how you're going to cope. The answer is: Finally, from henceforth, go forward; furthermore, be strong in the Lord. It was not until I got to this "final" point in my marriage that God was able to work. Before, I thought it was something that I could do. Not! It was a matter of my allowing God to be God and effect a change in both José and me.

To be "strong in the Lord" means to be empowered, be enabled, be activated for good works. This power we are talking about is taken from the Greek word that means "that awesome power." It's where we get the word "dynamite." So when the Bible tells us to be "strong in the Lord," it is talking about dynamite power. With God's power, you can blow the situation wide open.

We are told to be strong in the Lord for a reason. You know that when you're trying to do anything in your own strength, you just become tired; and when you get tired, distressed, or fed up, the weight is more than you can carry. But the Lord's power is mighty. The Lord does not get tired. When you have the Lord living within you (because of your relationship with Him) and you are growing spiritually because you are studying the Word and praying on a daily basis, you can rest in the Lord and work in His power. You can be strong because it's not in your strength that you continue; it's in the Lord's strength that you can carry on.

MY STORY

God has done wondrous works in my marriage. It is His power active and available in my life, in my marriage, and in my home that enables me to write this book. Sometimes I stop and look back, and I just do not believe it. I know it is the grace of God that has brought me through. As you read my story, think about your situation and how this information or my experience applies to you. Information is great, but it is no good if it is not applied and acted upon. So after reading, ask yourself: What can I do differently?

My husband and I have been married now for seventeen years, and I have been saved for sixteen of those years. The first year of our marriage was like heaven; it was bliss! At the time, I knew about the Lord, but I did not have a relationship with Him. I knew enough to pray before I went to bed. I sent my tithes to the local church and I knew that God was good, but that was about it.

I married a wonderful guy. My husband is an excellent cook. He put dinner on the table every night. I worked in corporate America. My colleagues could not believe that I left work and went home to candlelight dinners every night. But it was true. (I have often said that his mother could be Suzy Homemaker's sister—which would make my husband Suzy Homemaker's nephew.)

He also keeps an immaculate house. So not only would I come home to dinner by candlelight, but the house would be spotless. Many times, my bathwater would be drawn because he knew I had a long, hard day. I thought, "Wow, isn't this wonderful?"

At my job, there was a lady who was always going on and on about these miracles at her church. I kept thinking, "Yeah, yeah, I know God is good. I don't need to go to church. I am too busy. I have all of this work to do on the weekends. I don't have time for church." But she insisted, and finally I went to church with her. That evening, they were having testimony time during communion, and everybody was standing up talking about how good God was. So, I said, "OK, I know God. I can stand up and give a testimony too."

So I stood up and I went on and on about how great my life was, how wonderful my husband was, the delicious dinners on the table, and how I had this great job in corporate America making lots of money. I had just purchased a new home, a new car, and a new wardrobe for my upcoming travels. I had everything in life someone my age could possibly want. But there was still something missing and I was not sure what it was. At that point I began to get tears in my eyes. With all these wonderful things, I was still not happy. I quickly composed myself. Tears did not go with the executive image; everything would be OK. I would get to heaven and Peter would greet me at the gate and say, "Well, Sabrina, why should you come in?" And I would say, "Well, I sent my money to the church, and I sang in the choir and I served on the usher board. I am a pretty good person, people like me and I do good deeds most of the time." But somehow I wasn't sure if that would be enough. So I sat down and consoled myself by thinking, "That was a good testimony."

After service, about five people rushed me. I thought, "What? What did I do? What did I say?" And the lady who had invited me leaned over and said, "I will talk to her." I asked, "What did I do?" She said, "First of all, Sabrina, Peter will not greet you at the gate. And if you really want to go to heaven, all you have to do is believe on the Lord Jesus Christ, receive Him into your heart, and have faith that you will be there with Him in heaven." I thought, "That's all?"

After we prayed and I asked Jesus to be my Lord and Savior, the joy of the Lord bubbled over in my soul. I was so excited. I went home and I thought, "Great! I can't wait until I tell my husband the good news. I have found a Savior like no other." Then I remembered that he was not real keen on religion. It had never been a concern before because neither of us went to church (except for the holidays).

My husband grew up Catholic. He went to Mass regularly. He prayed the rosary, paid penance, went to see the priest—the whole nine yards. His father was a devout Catholic. My husband grew up hating religion. Later he tried to give religion a second chance, but he had a few bad experiences with the church. So he hated religion, and he hated churches. In spite of the importance of my great news, I began to think, "Maybe I shouldn't tell him just yet."

So, I had this wonderful secret, this newfound love that I was holding, just waiting for the right time to tell him. My girlfriend called and asked my husband, "Hey, did Sabrina tell you about her great news?" I had not told him yet. My husband's sarcastic response was, "So you joined the local church, huh?" I could tell by his comment that he wasn't pleased and that my not telling him sooner was a problem. I immediately began to highlight all the positive aspects of my joining the church. "Honey, it's a wonderful place," I said. "You would love these people. They're young and vibrant, college-educated like we are, and they have great jobs. Many are newlyweds and starting families. Come on, come on, you'll really like it." He grunted. His response was less than enthusiastic, but he did come to church a few times in those early years. I thought he would see for himself that it was OK and the people were not that bad. He even met several people he knew from college. And I thought excitedly, "Great, he will come back. Yes, he'll come back."

My husband did not come back, but I kept going. For me it was more than the church; it was my commitment to Christ. The love of the Lord was growing in my heart. I had a desire for God's Word, and I wanted to know how He would have me to live my life. I rushed to church every time they opened up the doors. Then I would go home and say, "Honey, guess what the pastor said . . ." "Do you know what the pastor said?" "And the Bible says . . ." "And the pastor said . . ." Not only did he hate religion, he hated the church, and now he hated the pastor. I kept thinking, "Lord, what am I doing wrong? I just love You so much, and I want him to come to know You, too." That was our second year of our marriage.

The days of bliss became a faint memory. We spent the next ten years trying to learn how to relate to each other all over again. We did not seem to have anything in common. The things that excited me when we were first married did not work anymore. When I accepted Christ in my life, I did a complete turnabout. The things I used to do or wanted to do, I had no desire for anymore.

Some of you may remember that when you first got saved, you became totally righteous—radically saved. As a new Christian, you knew all of the right things to do, all of the right answers, and all of the biblical approaches to life. I went home with that kind of attitude. However, I was totally self-righteous—a major sin, but I was too immature in my faith at the time to know it. So every time my husband did something wrong, he heard: "You're going to hell." "God will get you for that." "Let me show you how you ought to live."

Then I started leaving tracts in his lunch box, Bibles under his pillow, little notes and Scriptures posted on all of the mirrors and the refrigerator. For a nonbeliever it was Scripture overload. Can you imagine what a delight I was to live with? I often look back with wonder, and I know it must have been because of the grace of God that we are still married years later. The Lord knows I did not intend to, but I almost messed it up, by trying to help God save my husband.

WARNINGS AND REMINDERS

There are a couple of things I want to mention as precautions at this point. Most women who are involved in unequally yoked relationships have heard the Scripture that your husband may be won through your quiet and gentle spirit. "Wives, in the same way be submissive to your husbands so that, if any of them do not believe the word, they may be won over without words by the behavior of their wives" (1 Peter 3:1 NIV). My caution is that Scripture says that he *may* be won, not he *will* be won. It does not say that because you are quiet, gentle, and meek your husband will be saved in two weeks or any specific time frame. As a counselor, I see a lot of women who are carrying anxiety and guilt about their husband's salvation. However, we must remember that there was a time in our lives when we were without God and didn't know enough to know *we needed salvation.* Even if we knew, we could not save ourselves; and we certainly cannot save anyone else. Do not become burdened or feel responsible for your spouse's salvation. I know you probably don't fully believe that things will ever change. So go ahead, take matters into your own hands, tell him what he's missing, brag about what the pastor says, and what so-and-so's husband is doing! And after you have wasted your time doing these things—and it is a gross waste of time—trust in the Lord to draw your husband into the faith the same way that He drew us.

The second thing that we need to remember is that we are all sinners. Yet, God loves us and Christ died for us even while we were sinners. That is the way we *should* love our spouses. We should not be waiting for them to change, waiting for them to be fixed like a broken watch, or waiting for them to get saved before we show them the love of Christ. What happens is that in our zeal to get our husbands saved, we do everything but show the love of Christ. The fruit of the Spirit (love, joy, peace, patience, etc.) is totally absent from the picture. In our efforts to be his savior, the fruit of the Spirit is not perfected in our lives. Although you really want to "be all that," you still have growing to do. So stop thinking that you are better than your spouse—he can see right through you!—and your superior attitude does not provide a warm welcome.

My girlfriend Dee can tell this story better than I can. She confided that early in her marriage to Robert, she discovered that he did not want to go to Bible study every week. Well, this was "unacceptable" behavior for *her* husband, and she made her thoughts about it clear to him. What she realized later (after many arguments) was that her disappointment in Robert had to do with her grandiose perception of her own spirituality. She apologized to him for trying to make a clone of him. Well, guess what? God moved in his life and he began attending Bible study regularly and without her prodding form of "encouragement."

Remember, whenever two people are teamed together in marriage and are unequally yoked spiritually, they both will have a difficult time when one partner tries to pull toward the Lord. Also, keep in mind that the purpose of the yoke was to make the work easier. When you are not on the same page spiritually, one person is doing twice as much work.

When I understood this truth, I stopped asking, "Why do I have to do everything?" "Why do I have to be the spiritual giant?" (I really wasn't a spiritual giant; I just thought I was!) "Lord, why can't I get any help?" I realized that it was the work times two. I was carrying the burden for two people. This did not mean that I carried out my husband's responsibilities in other areas, but I did have to lead the family on a spiritual journey because I was the one who *knew* the Lord (and the way). But when I allowed the Lord to help me carry the burden, the journey was no longer full of tedium. It became a joy because I had help. I no longer did the work times two. It was, now, me and the Lord carrying the burden. That was God's desire for me; it is God's desire for you as well. Remember Matthew 11:29?

So I tell you that God is able. I know He can; I have watched Him do it. It is fourteen years later, and my husband and I have worked through so many issues. It's not easy by any means; often, it is very, very difficult. But I have a God who is mighty in power. It is His strength working in me that enables me to move forward.

No matter what your situation is, you can change. Furthermore, you now have the power of God active and available in your life to make a difference. As you focus on God, it changes your perspective on what you have been dealing with at home. You can change, whatever the situation. Even though it's been difficult, it's been hard, even when it seems impossible to go on, you can still do it with God's power alongside you. From this point forward, my brethren (my sisters), be strong in the Lord. No matter what you are doing or facing now, you have an opportunity to change. God's power is truly active and available if you allow Him to work in and through you. You can make the difference in your household.

THE FRUIT OF THE SPIRIT

It is the fruit of the Spirit growing in you that will enable you to move forward in an unequally yoked relationship. Galatians 5:22–23 says that the fruit of the Spirit is "love, joy, peace, patience, kindness, goodness, faithfulness, gentleness and self-control."

Take a personal inventory. As you look at the following list, take a moment to put little "plus" signs next to the fruit of the Spirit you feel you have in abundance. For example, if you feel like you are full of love, that you know how to love the unlovely, and you show unconditional love, put your plus there. If you look at the word *goodness* and you know that you are unselfish, always sharing, and always giving, put your plus there.

Do not go through the list and put a plus next to every character trait. Mark only the fruit that you honestly feel you have in abundance, those that the Lord has really ministered to you or anointed you in a certain area.

Then identify the areas where you struggle—places where you just really have a hard time. Find at least one or two character traits and put minuses next to them. A minus denotes qualities you wish to demonstrate, but you just can't seem to find in yourself.

- *Love* −
- *Joy*
- *Peace* −
- *Patience*
- *Kindness*
- *Goodness* −
- *Faithfulness* −
- *Gentleness* −
- *Self-control* −

There is one thing we need to remember about the fruit of the Spirit: it is God-given. It isn't something that we have to manufacture. We shouldn't have to muster up some faithfulness. Faithfulness is already in you, because the Spirit of the Lord is in you. The key is that we will become fruitful (even in areas where you indicated a minus) if we are growing. The critical question is: Are you growing in that area?

"According as his divine power hath given unto us all things that pertain unto life and godliness, through the knowledge of him that hath called us to glory and virtue" (2 Peter 1:3 KJV). When you became a new creature in Christ, you received everything you need for life and godliness. Although we are changed, we are babies in Christ. Babies need food to grow. You help your born-again spirit to grow by feeding it spiritual nourishment. You need to study the Word regularly; you need to be on your knees in prayer regularly. These are the things that will help your spirit to grow.

Look at each fruit of the Spirit. Note those you marked, but remember that when you are not growing in the Lord and walking in the Spirit, you will demonstrate the opposite negative characteristics.

Love. Whenever you are not demonstrating agape love, you are resentful, you have a critical spirit, and your love is conditional. Read 1 Corinthians 13:1–7, then think about what you marked and whether these are the attitudes you exhibit.

Though I speak with the tongues of men and of angels, and have not charity, I am become as sounding brass, or a tinkling cymbal. And though I have the gift of prophecy, and understand all mysteries, and all knowledge; and though I have all faith, so that I could remove mountains, and have not charity, I am nothing. And though I bestow all my goods to feed the poor, and though I give my body to be burned, and have not charity, it profiteth me nothing. Charity suffereth long, and is kind; charity envieth not; charity vaunteth not itself, is not puffed up, Doth not behave itself unseemly, seeketh not her own, is not easily provoked, thinketh no evil; Rejoiceth not in iniquity, but rejoiceth in the truth; Beareth all things, believeth all things, hopeth all things, endureth all things. (KJV)

Early in my marriage, my love was conditional. I knew that I was supposed to love my husband unconditionally, the way that Christ loved me. On the days that he responded the way that I wanted him to, I was a very loving wife. On the days that he did not, I had a major attitude problem. My love was conditional, although I knew better.

Joy. Scripture talks about the joy of your salvation. "Restore unto me the joy of thy salvation; and uphold me with thy free spirit" (Psalm 51:12 KJV). It is knowing Christ and His fullness that gives us joy. Our joy comes in knowing that we have a heavenly Father, and that we have the Holy Spirit who is aware of our infirmities and makes intercession on our behalf. This kind of joy does not come from your situation; it does not come from your circumstances. Knowing Christ is where the joy comes from, not from what is going on around you. Do not focus on what's going on around you. Just take a quick look at your situation, then fix your gaze upon God. You should be looking up. "I will lift up mine eyes unto the hills, from whence cometh my help" (Psalm 121:1 KJV). That is where your help comes from. That is where your joy is found.

In the Amplified Bible, Psalm 5:11 says, "But let all those who take refuge and put their trust in You rejoice; let them ever sing and shout for joy, because You make a covering over them and defend them; let those also who love Your name be joyful in You and be in high spirits." Note the phrase "in high spirits." It did not say moping around, depressed, or upset because things are not going your way. You should be glad and optimistic.

Peace. It is hard to be at peace when things are disorganized. When your household is not in order, it is difficult to have peace. God is not the author of confusion. "For God is not the author of confusion, but of peace, as in all churches of the saints" (1 Corinthians 14:33 KJV). So there can be no rest in that kind of chaotic situation. If you are restless, you are not at peace. If there is always confusion and conflict, you are not at peace. So don't fool yourself. Remember that you can have the peace of God that passes all understanding, even in the middle of a storm. "And the peace of God, which passeth all understanding, shall keep your hearts and minds through Christ Jesus" (Philippians 4:7 KJV). But if there is strife or confusion, then you are not at peace.

Patience. It is interesting to me whenever I hear people say, "Have the patience of Job." This advice sounds nice until you read Job's story. Job lived through a lot. I recently read a book that talks about Job's wife. You never really hear much about Job's wife, but she was catching it too. After all she lived through, at the end of the story, she dies. To have the patience of Job means you are going through one thing, after another, after another. My situation has never been as bad as Job's. So it is comparatively easy for me to be patient. It has been bad, and I have wanted to cancel some things out, but my situation is not that bad.

Kindness. If you are hard-hearted, if you are insensitive, unsympathetic, or sarcastic about everything, do not claim to be kind. My husband used to tell me (during our third year of marriage) that it was really interesting how quick-witted I was. That was his way of saying that I was sarcastic. I know how to use words, and I can say things that hurt. My husband would get his verbal jabs in, and I would go into the bathroom crying. By the time I finished wiping my eyes, I would come out fueled up and ready to fight, and I would hit below the belt. I would be very sarcastic—not kind at all, not gentle, not meek, nor humble. How could I feel like I was flowing in the fruit of the Spirit and that I was living for the Lord? I had to learn how to tame my tongue if I was going to truthfully say I was living for the Lord. I found that the tongue is difficult to tame. It took the power of God—active and available—to stop my tongue from wagging. Scripture admonishes us in Romans 12:1 to present our bodies (including our tongues) a living sacrifice, holy and acceptable unto the Lord.

Goodness. Goodness has to do with giving and being generous, and not being stingy and self-centered. The world does not revolve around me, although I used to think so. I thought that if my husband were saved my whole world would change; his new life in Christ would offer opportunities for me. Unfortunately, the world does not revolve around me. There are other issues, there are other life stories, and there are other story lines. Each of our lives has a story line. We may often feel like ours is the worst or the most important. That is not the case. I am sure all of us have war stories that we could tell. And even though I know how much I have lived through, I probably have not lived through half as much as some of you. But the world does not revolve around us. Therefore, when you pray, do not just pray for your situation; pray for the situations of other men and women who are in unequally yoked marriages. Pray for help for them in their trials and tribulations. Pray for your spouse and yourself—you both really need prayer. You have been saved by the grace of God. You already know the Lord; your spouse is the one who needs to come to know Him. So pray for him or her as you would pray for yourself.

Faithfulness. Faithfulness in God means that you know that His Word is true beyond a shadow of a doubt, and you trust the Lord to do what He says He will do. If you are always worrying, you cannot be trusting God. If you are always compromising your beliefs and your values, then you are not trusting God. If you are always fearful of what might happen, then you cannot be filled with faith. When I was afraid to tell my husband that I was saved, I was not having faith in God. I was not counting on God to work the situation out. My tendency was to always think three steps ahead: "Now, if I do this, he will do this; but if I do that, then he will do this. But then again, maybe I'll wait because I'm not sure how he is going to respond, and he catches me off guard all of the time." This is a good example of what you are not supposed to say and what you are not supposed to do. I wanted to be prepared for each possible response. But I needed to learn to be faithful toward God, to wait on Him, and to know that He would do the things He said He would do. I had to learn to be faithful just to do my part—not try to do everybody else's.

Gentleness. Gentleness is manifested in our lives through a teachable spirit. When we open ourselves to the ways of God, He will teach us that His ways are above our ways. Gentleness places itself in submission to the ways and laws of God and humbly considers others above itself. When this fruit manifests itself in marriage, both parties benefit greatly. Gentleness teaches us how to return good for evil. It confidently rests in the Lord. Its prayer is "I must decrease, You must increase. Not my will, but Yours be done." As we move ourselves out of the way, the Spirit of God takes control. It's the thing miracles are made of. If you want to see God show up in your situation, eat the fruit of gentleness.

Self-control. I always wondered why self-control was at the end of the list. It should be at the beginning because self-control is something that we often lack. We usually believe that we can demonstrate the other fruits of the Spirit. We think it is easier; but because we lack self-control, we find it more difficult than we imagined. We have not yet learned how to control our tongues, our actions, and our attitudes. Scripture talks about taking every thought into captivity. "Casting down imaginations, and every high thing that exalteth itself against the knowledge of God, and bringing into captivity every thought to the obedience of Christ" (2 Corinthians 10:5 KJV). Some of the thoughts about what you are going to do—what you would do if—should be taken captive instead of acted upon. We need to exercise more self-control in our lives and our marriages.

CHANGING OUR PERSPECTIVE

The Lord is constantly revealing what is going on in our lives. When we really draw near and get close to God, we will become so empowered that we will not be discouraged by what is going on around us. We begin to understand that He can cause it to work together to accomplish His purpose. When we focus on God, we will see that He is up to something and that He wants to use us. We can become His instrument, useful in the hand of the Master, as we take part in His work. And that is such an awesome, awesome place to be.

When we change our perspective, we will also realize that we are at war. We are warring for our marriages. We need to be wise. Satan wants to steal our peace and joy, destroy our marriage and our testimony. Scripture says that we should not be ignorant of Satan's devices. "Lest Satan should get an advantage of us: for we are not ignorant of his devices" (2 Corinthians 2:11 KJV). But it is the power of God active and available and the fruit of the Spirit growing in us that enables us to move forward to obtain and maintain all that God has for us.

Ephesians 6:10–13 says, "Finally, my brethren, be strong in the Lord, and in the power of his might. Put on the whole armour of God, that ye may be able to stand against the wiles of the devil. For we wrestle not against flesh and blood, but against principalities, against powers, against the rulers of the darkness of this world, against spiritual wickedness in high places. Wherefore take unto you the whole armour of God, that ye may be able to withstand in the evil day, and having done all, to stand" (KJV).

"STAND." That is what we need to do, and that is what we must help others to do as well. Your marriage may be bad, but it is not the worst marriage. You can stand, and you do not have to stand alone. You don't have to stand on your own. It is the power of God active and available in you that helps you to stand. In your own energy and strength, you just can't do it. In your own energy and strength, you can't love your spouse unconditionally. In your own energy and strength, you won't want to stay in a situation that you view as negative. This is an opportunity for you to fight the good fight. God in you enables you and empowers you to stand.

God will give you power to deal with today. Remember, you are there for a reason. God desires to work some things in you and through you. You can complete the work He has given you to do in His strength, in His might. "For it is God which worketh in you both to will and to do of his good pleasure" (Philippians 2:13 KJV).

Let us pray.

> *Heavenly Father, I thank You so much for the women and men who are reading this. You know our situations. You know our hurts and our pains. Lord, I pray that You will help us endure to the end.*
>
> *Father, we thank You for Your magnificence, for Your glory. Lord, I thank You for Your power and how You enable us to carry on. I pray that our lives would be changed by Your power and that we would listen clearly for the message from You. Help us to be strong in You and share Your message and become a beacon of hope to others.*
>
> *Dear Lord, we pray for our spouses. We know that it is Your desire that none should perish, and that all should come to the saving knowledge of Your grace. That they would come to know You and grow in You, Father, is our prayer. It is in the Lord Jesus' name that we pray. Amen.*

CHAPTER TWO

What Does It Mean to Be Unequally Yoked?

It is important to establish what it means to be unequally yoked. When we discuss unequally yoked marriages, what are we actually talking about? The verb "to yoke" means to unite or to connect. Webster's Dictionary defines a yoke as an apparatus used to bind two separate things together.

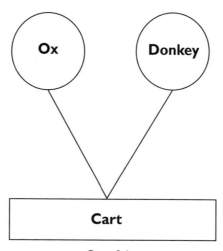

Figure 2-1

In agrarian societies, a yoke was commonly used in farming to bind two animals together for work. For example, a farmer typically joined a pair of oxen, mules, or horses together by a yoke around their necks. The pair then pulled a big plow attached behind them to turn the ground and   cultivate the soil. In the Bible, a yoke was often used to bind donkeys, mules, or oxen together to pull a plow or a cart.

The purpose of the yoke was to produce the work times two. When you have more than one doing the work, more can be accomplished. In other words, a team or pair can complete the work quickly and easily when they are compatible and pull together in the same direction. The team will have twice the strength and stability.

UNEQUALLY YOKED RELATIONSHIPS

Being in an unequally yoked relationship often means that one person is not helping to pull. Are you trying to figure out why you have to carry so much responsibility or why there is so much work for you to do? It is because *you* are doing the work times two. This realization helped me to stop asking: "Why do I have to do everything?" The answer was simple: "Because I am unequally yoked." This ox (my husband) was pulling in another direction.

Whenever people or animals are unequally yoked, there are problems. Imagine some of the problems that might occur as a result of connecting two obviously different animals together. For example, suppose you have an ox and a donkey, and you want to yoke them together. An ox is much stronger than a donkey. The types of things the donkey feeds on would make an ox sick to the stomach. Their legs are different sizes, so one animal would take bigger strides and move at a faster pace than the other.

Because of the way a yoke is designed, when the pair or team does not work together the yoke is tightened. Whenever the donkey moves ahead of the ox, the weight of the ox would cause the donkey to choke. Similarly, the forward motion of the donkey would choke the ox as it is dragged along at a pace that it is unprepared to go. Because of their yoke, both the animal being pulled and the one doing the pulling would begin to choke. In fact, the Bible also says, "Do not plow with an ox and a donkey yoked together" (Deuteronomy 22:10 NIV). Because the two animals are dissimilar, they cannot move at the same pace, and they will not be able to accomplish the same types of things.

This also happens in unequally yoked marriages. Whenever one of you is growing and the other is stagnant, you will find that you are pulling and tugging on each other. Besides being spiritually unbalanced, you may be unbalanced in other areas as well. For example, you may be unequally yoked in politics, education, personal virtues and values, social skills, etc. However, the focus of this book is on the marital imbalance that results when believers are married to unbelievers. As the two of you start to move forward, the one who knows the Lord will try to pull the other person along. This can cause pain for the person who is being pulled, as well as for the one who is doing the pulling because it chokes and stifles the relationship.

In this unbalanced relationship, your freedom in Christ is somewhat restricted because of the marital yoke. You will find that you are trying to pull and forge ahead in a direction that your spouse may not want to go personally nor have the household go. As a result, there may be some things that you really want to do that are difficult or impossible because you are unequally yoked.

For example, Wesley and Mae had been married for sixteen years when Mae decided that she did not want their children to be raised in a housing project. Besides, she insisted, they could afford a home. Wesley, on the other hand, did not see the need to move because he was looking at the financial savings of living in a low-income area. However, Mae knew that the environment was not the best for "her" children and insisted until he agreed to begin the search for a home.

Wesley initially resented Mae for increasing his financial burden. And since they were "her" children, he let her raise them without his input for the first four years after they moved. Now, some thirty years later, Wesley doesn't recall the turmoil. He just credits his wife with the foresight to move into a home, which he has since paid off.

We were not designed to do all the work by ourselves. Besides, each of us brings special gifts/strengths to the marital union that help to make the marriage a whole one. But when we fail to see how our spouse enhances the quality of the marriage, we find ourselves out of sync, pulling in opposing directions, and we remain uneven and stressed. In the Bible, we discover that the marital union is God's idea. Since God devised this plan for our lives, there must be a way to work out or even out our differences so that we can realize the words in the following Scriptures:

Genesis 2:24: *Therefore shall a man leave his father and his mother, and shall cleave unto his wife: and they shall be one flesh.*

Matthew 19:4–6: *And he answered and said unto them, Have ye not read, that he which made them at the beginning made them male and female, And said, For this cause shall a man leave father and mother, and shall cleave to his wife: and they twain shall be one flesh? Wherefore they are no more twain, but one flesh. What therefore God hath joined together, let not man put asunder.*

Ephesians 5:31: *For this cause shall a man leave his father and mother, and shall be joined unto his wife, and they two shall be one flesh.*

We are told in Scripture not to become unequally yoked. Paul admonished the Corinthian believers about marrying unbelievers because some of them were joining with the heathen in idolatrous feasts and other practices that would lead to their spiritual decline. He wrote, "Be ye not unequally yoked with unbelievers: for what fellowship hath righteousness with unrighteousness? And what communion hath light with darkness?" (2 Corinthians 6:14 KJV). How can two walk together unless they agree?

YOKES DEFINED IN SCRIPTURE

The Bible uses the word "yoke" both literally and figuratively. Scripture often calls the binding together of two separate things as "putting the yoke upon you." Yokes are used to describe oppression, hardship, submission, bondage, legalism, fellowship, discipleship, and marriage.

The yoke of oppression is described in Deuteronomy 28:48–68. In this biblical account, the children of Israel did not serve the Lord during the time of prosperity. They didn't fully rejoice in the things of God; therefore they were burdened with an iron yoke. Scripture describes how the yoke of oppression would destroy them; it would weigh them down because they would not serve the Lord.

The yoke of hardship is illustrated in 1 Kings 12:4–14 and 2 Chronicles 10:4–11. The children of Israel were asking King Rehoboam to ease the burden that his father had placed on them. They had been under a yoke of hardship due to slavery. They were trying to make an appeal, saying, "Please lighten our load." After considering their request, the king shook his head and said, "No way. If you think this is a heavy burden, wait until I really increase your labor." They were under a heavy yoke of hardship that became even more difficult.

The yoke of submission is found in Jeremiah 27:8–28:2. This passage speaks about bowing down under the rule of a king or an authority. When the children of Israel were under King Nebuchadnezzer, they had to bow and submit to whatever he said. They were under a yoke of submission because they were under the king's authority. Because of this yoke of submission, the Israelites were forced to revere and obey the king of Babylon. This is the same yoke that many women have been unjustly burdened with. Even when physically beaten or verbally abused, a person cannot be forced to reverence someone else. Submission is done willingly from the heart.

There is also a yoke of bondage to sin. It is often referred to as a "yoke of bondage," especially when we speak of addiction. A person may be in bondage to gambling, alcohol, drugs, or a sexual addiction. An example of the yoke of bondage is found in Lamentations 1:4–14. This passage describes how the heavy yoke of sin saps the strength of the people.

The yoke of legalism is illustrated in Galatians chapter 5. I think it's interesting that this chapter begins by telling us, "It is for freedom that Christ has set us free. Stand firm, then, and do not let yourselves be burdened again by a yoke of slavery" (v. 1 NIV). In other words, the Bible plainly admonishes us: "If Christ has made you free, do not let yourselves be yoked again in bondage. Do not even allow that to happen to you. Do not get tangled up again; refuse to become ensnared by the yoke of legalism." There are people who would try to yoke you with the letter of the Law, which would lead you back into bondage. The freedom that Christ has given allows you to embrace the spirit of the Law.

Three positive yokes found in the New Testament Scriptures are the yoke of fellowship, discipleship, and marriage. **The yoke of fellowship** involves being bonded together in friendship, companionship, brotherhood, partnership, or willing service. The yoke of fellowship between believers is described in Acts 2:42 and 2 Corinthians 8:4 KJV.

Acts 2:42: *And they continued steadfastly in the apostles' doctrine and fellowship, and in breaking of bread, and in prayers.*

2 Corinthians 8:4: *Praying us with much entreaty that we would receive the gift, and take upon us the fellowship of the ministering to the saints.*

The yoke that people are most familiar with is ***the yoke of discipleship*** that Jesus described in Matthew 11:28–30. Here, Jesus said that we should take His yoke upon us, because He is gentle and humble and we will find rest for our souls. We need His yoke; we are designed to take the yoke of discipleship to Christ upon us. The yoke of discipleship gives us power and rest. That is what we must understand and remember, even when we are in unequally yoked relationships. As we are yoked with the Lord Jesus Christ, our burden will indeed become light because His yoke is easy. It is through this yoke (our partnership with Christ) that we are able to survive, thrive, and be revived.

The yoke of marriage is referred to in 2 Corinthians 6:14. In this verse, the Bible teaches why we should not be unequally yoked. If more people understood the whole concept and definition of a yoke—including the yoke of hardship, the yoke of submission, and the yoke of sin—the biblical warning against being unequally yoked would make a lot more sense.

Without this understanding, hearing the admonition "Do not be unequally yoked" sounds irrelevant or old-fashioned. I have made this statement many times to people in counseling. Far too often, they respond by saying, "Oh, you just don't want me to be with this fun person." Or they may say to a friend, "You're just upset because you haven't found anyone," when, in fact, the Lord is trying to prevent them from having to do the work times two, being choked in the relationship, and dragging someone else along unwillingly. A clearer understanding of a yoke would help many single people decide to avoid unequally yoked relationships.

UNEQUALLY YOKED MARRIAGES

We find ourselves in unequally yoked relationships for different reasons. However, if you find yourself in an unequally yoked marriage, God has commanded that what He has joined together, let no man separate. "Wherefore they are no more twain, but one flesh. What therefore God hath joined together, let not man put asunder" (Matthew 19:6 KJV). Being unequally yoked is no reason to divorce or separate. What you must learn is how to grow even though the relationship is unbalanced.

Some of you have been yoked together with unbelievers because of rebellion. You just decided that you were going to do it anyway. He or she was a good person, who loved you, could provide for you or care for you, and you figured you would save him or her after you got married. The reality is that you can't save anyone, including yourself. So it was because of open rebellion that you now find yourself in this situation.

Others have situations similar to mine. You accepted Christ in your life after you were married. You thought that salvation would bring rejoicing and excitement into your home, not the strife that it appears to have caused between you and your spouse. I say "appears" because it is a matter of perspective. The tension may be the conflict between light and darkness. We may view our salvation as the cause of conflict, when in reality it may be: our immaturity in the faith, our own self-righteous behavior, our misinterpretation of Scripture, or our immature or inappropriate responses in various situations. It may also be our spouse's unbiblical response to change.

There are primarily three different types of unequally yoked marriages:

- *only one spouse is saved,*

- *spouses are of different religions, or*

- *one spouse is growing spiritually (and in other areas) and their partner is standing still.*

You may find yourself in one of these three situations, or you may know someone who is.

The first type of unequally yoked marriage—where only one spouse has a religious affiliation—is the one that most people are familiar with. You have a relationship with Jesus Christ as your Lord and Savior and your spouse does not.

The second type involves a marriage where the husband and wife have different beliefs or religious backgrounds. For example, one spouse may be Catholic and the other Muslim. They are not pulling towards the same Lord or the same goal. One may be Jewish and the other Christian. They are unequally yoked. The couple may be unequally yoked because they are members of different denominations. One person may be a traditional Southern Baptist and the other may be Holiness Pentecostal. They have the same Lord, but there are differences in doctrinal focus and practice.

The third type of unequally yoked marriage is commonly overlooked. It relates to spouses who are at different levels of spiritual maturity. Some people accept Jesus Christ as their Savior because they do not want to go to hell. They get saved, but they never grow spiritually. They do not mature in the things of God. They are content to live at a level that says Jesus as Savior is sufficient. In contrast, many others are learning to live a life of submission and commitment to Jesus Christ as Savior *and* Lord. Their desire is to live in a way that says, "Christ is indeed the Lord of my life; He rules, He reigns."

Oftentimes, Christians who are married to other Christians have a hard time identifying or find it difficult to understand that they may still be unequally yoked. You may have heard the questions: "I have accepted God and I know I'm going to heaven; isn't that enough?" "Why do I need to go to church on a regular basis?" "Why do we have to look in the Bible to figure out how to do things?" "Why do I need to give away my money?" "What do you mean you want me to give 10 percent of our money?" "Why do we have to raise our children or do things in a certain way?" These questions may be indicative of an unequally yoked relationship.

Remember the example of the ox and the donkey? Now imagine some of the problems that could occur in an unequally yoked Christian marriage. Again, both have different ways of looking at things and different approaches to getting the work done. For example, one spouse says, "This is how we are to manage our finances." The other spouse says, "No, no, no! This is how we need to manage our finances." One says, "This is what God said; we give the 10 percent first." The other says, "No, we pay bills first. And if there is anything left over, maybe you can give some to your preacher and to your church." One spouse may say, "This is the way we need to raise our children." The other says, "No, we need to raise our children in the Spirit and admonition of the Lord." And so it goes, from child rearing to finances, from vacation to vocation and recreation. There is no common understanding or agreement on how they will live. Every area of life and everything that a couple does is impacted by whether or not they are unequally yoked.

"Can two walk together except they agree?" (Amos 3:3 paraphrased). The two can learn to agree, but it takes time, it takes an act of the will, and it takes God.

Dee and Robert struggled with the issue of giving the tithe. He wanted to give to the Lord first and she wanted to pay the bills. She went along with her spouse and reports that they have never suffered because of it. In fact, she reports that God has blessed them with an abundance.

EQUAL YOKES

When a Christian couple is equally yoked, the evidence can be seen in the things to which they are committed. It is like four concentric circles. Both partners have:

1. **P**rofessed faith in Christ
2. **C**ommitted to the lordship of Christ
3. **C**ommitted to the biblical order of marriage
4. **C**ommitted to biblical problem solving

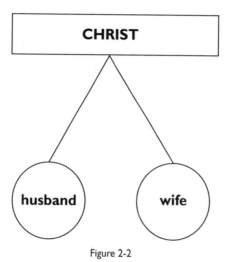

Figure 2-2

If your marriage does not fit this illustration, then there is an imbalance. Both partners should be pulling in the same direction—toward the Lord.

GOD'S YOKE IS EASY

God's design for marriage is that the two would be yoked together spiritually and that the yoke would be inverted so that Christ becomes the focal point.

As the husband and wife draw closer to the Lord, they will draw closer to each other. So, as you and your spouse grow spiritually, both of you are growing closer together because you are growing closer to the Lord. If you have spent time close up with an equally yoked couple, you may have noticed that they almost move as one.

Dee and Robert have been married for twenty years and the bond that they have exudes togetherness. In social situations, they not only talk to others, but they talk to each other—a sure sign of oneness. Similarly, Anne and Miguel, in an effort to reduce marital discord, vowed that whenever they played games in social situations that they would always be on the same team. However, when it is impossible for them to side together, one inevitably helps the other—much to the dismay of their teammates. These couples have grown together and have a peace about them that passes understanding.

God's goal is that we will be yoked together—teamed—with Him. God's plan is that a man and woman who are joined together in marriage will be drawn toward Him—that they will pull together toward Him, and He will pull together *with* them. As husbands and wives, our goal is to be yoked together with the Lord.

Jesus invites us in Scripture to "take my yoke upon you, and learn of me; for I am meek and lowly in heart: and ye shall find rest unto your souls. For my yoke is easy, and my burden is light" (Matthew 11:29–30 KJV). As we are yoked together with the Lord, we have the almighty God helping us to pull the load, to do the work, to carry the burden. Now the work times two becomes very light and very easy because God is helping us complete the work.

Let's pray.

> *Dear Lord, Thank You for Your Word that teaches us of Your perfect love. You have written Your Word as a gift so we may live the abundant life. We desire to walk in the way that You have ordered. We confess that our marriages have knowingly or unknowingly failed to line up with Your Word. We submit our marriages to You. Have Your way as we learn to willingly wear Your yoke and move forward in Your grace. In Jesus' name we pray. Amen.*

CHAPTER THREE

Walking in Wisdom

Wisdom is the key to a balanced Christian walk. In an unbalanced or unequally yoked relationship, wisdom is our foundation. Therefore, it is extremely important that in all of our getting, we get wisdom and understanding to apply in our marriages.

THE IMPORTANCE OF WISDOM

Scripture emphasizes the importance of wisdom. It tells why we should seek wisdom and how God will give knowledge and understanding. In an unequally yoked relationship, we need a lot of wisdom, a lot of knowledge, and a lot of understanding because as we grow spiritually we must avoid choking our partner and stifling their growth. Our spiritual growth should not cause them to stumble.

We receive wisdom from the Word of God. The following verses reveal the importance of wisdom (unless indicated, all verses quoted in this chapter are taken from the Amplified Bible).

Proverbs 2:1–10: *My son, [my daughter,] if you will receive my words and treasure up my commandments within you, making your ear attentive to skillful and godly Wisdom and inclining and directing your heart and mind to understanding [applying all of your powers to the quest for it]; yes, if you cry out for insight and raise your voice for understanding, if you seek [Wisdom] as for silver and search for skillful and godly Wisdom as for hidden treasures, then you will understand the reverent and worshipful fear of the Lord and find the knowledge of [our omniscient] God. For the Lord gives skillful and godly Wisdom; from His mouth come knowledge and understanding. He hides away sound and godly Wisdom and stores it for the righteous (those who are upright and in right standing with Him); He is a shield to those who walk uprightly and in integrity, that He may guard the path of justice; yes, He preserves the way of His saints. Then you will understand righteousness, justice, and fair dealing [in every area and relation]; yes, you will understand every good path. For skillful and godly Wisdom shall enter into your heart, and knowledge shall be pleasant to you.*"

Proverbs 3:13–15: *Happy (blessed, fortunate, enviable) is the man who finds skillful and godly Wisdom, and the man who gets understanding [drawing it forth from God's Word and life's experiences], for the gaining of it is better than the gaining of silver, and the profit of it better than fine gold. Skillful and godly Wisdom is more precious than rubies; and nothing you can wish for is to be compared to her.*

Proverbs 4:4–7: *He taught me and said to me, Let your heart hold fast my words; keep my commandments and live. Get skillful and godly Wisdom, get understanding (discernment, comprehension, and interpretation); do not forget and do not turn back from the words of my mouth. Forsake not [Wisdom], and she will keep, defend, and protect you; love her, and she will guard you. . . . Get wisdom (skillful and godly Wisdom)! [For skillful and godly Wisdom is the principle thing.] And with all you have gotten, get understanding (discernment, comprehension, and interpretation).*

Proverbs 16:16: *How much better is it to get skillful and godly Wisdom than gold! And to get understanding is to be chosen rather than silver.*

Proverbs 24:3–4: *Through skillful and godly Wisdom is a house (a life, a home, a family) built, and by understanding it is established [on a sound and good foundation], And by knowledge shall its chambers [of every area] be filled with all precious and pleasant riches.*

James 1:5: *If any of you is deficient in wisdom, let him ask of the giving God [Who gives] to everyone liberally and ungrudgingly, without reproaching or faultfinding, and it will be given him.*

If you lack wisdom, ask.

To walk in wisdom, there are six key points to consider:

1. **W**alk your talk.

If you say you are a Christian, then allow Christ to live His life through you when you are at church as well as when you are at home. It will help if you learn how to walk your talk. We are challenged in God's Word (and the church covenant, too) to walk circumspectly, realizing that the world (especially your spouse) is watching. The people who live with us have an opportunity to witness how consistent we are in applying the principles we claim to believe.

2. **I**ntercede for your spouse and your marriage.

You should not pray only for yourself, but you should pray for your household. God has called us to a powerful ministry of prayer. When we are on our knees before the Lord lifting up our spouses, we are in a position to make a major impact in their lives.

3. **S**ubmit to your husband as unto the Lord.

Submission is for every Christian, not just for wives. It is not a bad word. Submission is a sign of growth and maturity. Learning to submit to your husband as unto the Lord can be a difficult process if you have had a bad experience or received negative messages about submission. But God is faithful. He will strengthen you and empower you to carry out His will. Sacrifice yourself for your spouse. Do this out of love as Christ loved the church.

4. **D**well with your spouse according to knowledge.

Whether you have been married for one year, ten years, or twenty years, you should know some things about the person you live with, such as what pleases and displeases them. So dwell with your spouse according to knowledge.

My husband is an extremely punctual person. Whatever the event, we are usually the first to arrive. This would often bother me. But I realized that I had choices. I could be glad he was going and be ready early; I could go when I wanted to and tell him not to accompany me; or I could not be ready early and know that he would be upset about being late. I know what he likes and how he responds. As I make my choice, I dwell according to knowledge.

5. **O**bey the Lord in all things, even the difficult things.

To obey the Lord in all things we must know what God requires of us. "To obey is better than sacrifice" (1 Samuel 15:22). However, God requires more than mere outward obedience; true obedience begins in the heart. As we live for God, we grow in our willingness to do those things that He requires of us: to seek forgiveness when we have caused an offense, to seek reconciliation, to love those who are unlovable.

6. **M**aintain the marriage as honorable and maintain a close relationship with the Lord.

As we align our priorities with the Word of God, we will begin to nurture and guard our two most important relationships: our spiritual relationship with the Lord and our marital relationship with our spouse.

Let us examine each point in detail.

WALK YOUR TALK

While it may be a challenge, it is indeed a high calling to be in an unequally yoked marriage. And I am the first to admit—I was not walking my talk. At least not according to Ephesians 4:1 where the Bible talks about walking worthy of the call: "I therefore, the prisoner for the Lord, appeal to and beg you to walk (lead a life) worthy of the [divine] calling to which you have been called [with behavior that is a credit to the summons to God's service]." To walk worthy of the call, you must know God's plan. What is God calling you to do? What has God designed for your life? To find out, you must spend time in His Word, time in fellowship with Him, and time in prayer listening to the Lord. Then you can walk worthy of the call.

In Colossians 1:10, it talks about walking pleasingly: "That ye might walk worthy of the Lord unto all pleasing, being fruitful in every good work, and increasing in the knowledge of God" (KJV). Doing what is pleasing to the Lord involves both attitude and action. It is often easy to do outward service with an unchanged heart. To please the Lord and to grow spiritually, you must change from the inside out. Ask the Lord to create in you a clean heart so that you can serve with genuine love and joy in the Lord and walk in a way that is pleasing to Him.

I wanted to make a difference in my household. I was going to convince my husband that being a Christian was the best thing for him and that he needed salvation right away. So I came home and did all of the good Christian things that a wife should do. I cooked meals seven days a week. I cleaned the house (the way he would) every day. I prayed every morning, and I left little notes in his lunch box with Scripture references on them. Oh, I also preached damnation and hellfire if he did not decide to accept Christ right away. I knew that God did not want any to perish without the saving knowledge of the Lord Jesus Christ.

In my own way, I was trying to encourage him, by doing what I thought would be pleasing to the Lord. But my heart was not right. I said, my heart was not right. (Can I get a witness!) I was doing it because I wanted to make life easier for myself. This is a hard truth. But, as they say, the truth is the light. Anyway, I wanted all of my blessings, spiritual and material, and thought that if he got saved I could get what was coming to me. I also rationalized that if my husband were saved, I would not have the pressure of hearing his comments about my new walk of faith. We could walk in faith together and encourage each other.

I can't tell you how many nights I spent in tears because I had cooked the perfect meal and he did not even come home in time to eat it. There were times that I cooked seven days in a row, which most of my friends know was a miracle for me. But all he would say was, "Yeah, OK, it was good." I wanted praise, excitement, and rejoicing. I'd been slaving to serve him. I thought this is what a Christian wife does: serve her husband. But all he said was, "Yeah, OK, you are supposed to cook; that's what wives do." He didn't realize what a labor of love this was for me; I was cooking and cleaning with all of my heart.

When my husband did not acknowledge what I thought was wonderful Christian service, I became depressed. I grew angry and bitter, and I was mad the next time I cooked. When I put dinner on the table, I was not happy about doing it because he did not acknowledge the last three meals that I had cooked.

Then the Lord changed my heart. I finally understood that my husband might never acknowledge anything that I do. I realized that I should have been doing those things for the Lord. The Lord would always be pleased with my service. My husband may or may not care, but God would. So it became a lot easier to go home and cook because it was what God would have me to do.

Some of you may be in two-career households where you do not have to rush home in the evening to cook a meal. Perhaps your spouse helps with the cooking and the cleaning; maybe you alternate days. Whatever your arrangement is, serve your spouse and the Lord with gladness. Whatever you do in your household should please the Lord. Do it for God and not your spouse. Then you will not be disappointed if your spouse does not acknowledge it. Whenever you serve others for the Lord, it makes serving much easier.

Keep in mind that as a Christian you should be Christlike. You must be willing to walk your talk. Don't say that you are a Christian and fail to live the Christian life or show the fruit of the Spirit. To walk your talk sounds easy, but it is not—especially when you have an unsaved spouse. Remember that the same grace that saved you needs to be applied to your unbalanced relationship. It's not easy, but it is possible with God. So wait, I say, on the Lord.

As a new believer, one of the things I learned right away was that my husband seemed to know more about the Bible than I did. When I messed up, he knew the principles that were violated. While I was still in transition, still learning how God would have me live, I had my husband right there watching and saying, "Hmm, Christians can do that, huh?" I had to stop and ask myself, "Well, can they?" At times, I was not sure what was acceptable behavior for Christians. But the Bible is very clear. The principles of the Bible are black and white. Through studying the Word of God, I was able to learn the Law and the spirit of the Law.

Those so-called gray areas are usually the places that cause others to stumble. The things that I thought were not a big deal were things that were causing my husband to stumble and to question my walk with Christ. As part of my spiritual growth and maturity, I learned to walk circumspectly, realizing there was someone in my household who was watching every move I made. Initially, this was a lot of pressure. I did not want him watching me, but I learned to appreciate it.

Think about how different your life would be if Jesus lived in your house. There is a poem that talks about what might happen if Jesus came to visit you for a day or two. Have you heard it? You know, the Bible would be laid out on the table, all the rooms would be clean, and everything would be holy, holy, holy. But the tendency at home is to relax—not that you are in sin, but you are relaxed because no one is watching.

I began to realize that I could not relax as much as I wanted to in my Christian walk. I had to be on guard, always ready to give an account for the hope that was in me, always showing a good example. That meant I needed to be in the Word a lot, I needed to be on my knees praying a lot, and I needed to be in fellowship with other believers. So the first point in your wisdom walk is to walk your talk. That is one of the best ways to exercise wisdom in an unequally yoked relationship.

Intercede for Your Spouse and Your Marriage

The second point is to intercede for your spouse and your marriage. Let's look at Romans 8:26. It says, "So too the [Holy] Spirit comes to our aid and bears us up in our weakness; for we do not know what prayer to offer nor how to offer it worthily as we ought, but the Spirit Himself goes to meet our supplication and pleads in our behalf with unspeakable yearnings and groanings too deep for utterance."

There were some nights that I had no idea what to pray. I would just fall on my knees and cry out to the Lord. This verse really ministered to me when I realized that I had One who was also inter-ceding on my behalf. It helped so much to know that the Holy Spirit groaned and interceded for me with utterances that were unspeak-able. Therefore, in light of the situation that you are dealing with—the trials, triumphs, challenges, or the level of pain that you face today—you need to fall on your knees before the Lord, ask the Holy Spirit to intercede for you, intercede for your marriage, and inter-cede for your spouse. I encourage you to pray, and pray, and pray without ceasing. It is so important that you build a foundation of prayer for your marriage.

Colossians 1:11 says, "[We pray] that you may be invigorated and strengthened with all power according to the might of His glory, [to exercise] every kind of endurance and patience (perseverance and forbearance) with joy." You can pray for strength and endurance. Pray that the fruit of the Spirit will be manifested in your life. As a new Christian, I was under the impression that I would sanctify my household; therefore my husband would be saved in a week or two—no more than a couple of months. Years later, I was still pray-ing and interceding, so I needed much patience and much forbear-ance. Here are some suggested areas for which you can pray: your strength, your patience, your spouse, your marriage, and other unequally yoked couples.

Some of our situations are far beyond us and beyond our abil-ity to change; but it is exciting to know that we serve an awesome God. When we look back after our God has brought us through, we will be truly amazed. I can say, "Great is God's faithfulness," because I know where I have been, and I know how far He has brought me. There were times in our marriage when in my mind I was ready to leave, and I'm sure there were times when my hus-band may have wanted me to leave. I had beaten him so badly with the Bible that he was probably saying, "Take the Bible and go."

Scripture says if the unbelieving spouse wants to leave, let him go. "But if the unbelieving partner [actually] leaves, let him do so;

in such [cases the remaining] brother or sister is not morally bound. But God has called us to peace" (1 Corinthians 7:15). However, it does not say put him out. I wanted to put him out. I said, "You are not a believer, and I am a believer, and this is not going to work. We are both struggling. Why don't you go ahead and pack? God will understand." But that is not what the Scripture teaches. It says, if he wants to leave, it is OK to let him go. It did not say make him leave, encourage him to go, or tell him all of the reasons why the marriage won't work. Instead, you should be praying that God would move in the heart of your spouse, as well as in your marriage, and that He would strengthen you—give you endurance, patience, and forbearance.

Even in prayer, our endeavor is to become more and more like Christ. Hebrews 7:25 says, "Therefore He is able also to save to the uttermost (completely, perfectly, finally, and for all time and eternity) those who come to God through Him, since He is always living to make petition to God and intercede with Him and intervene for them." It is God who is able to save. The Spirit makes intercession and intervenes. So we pray in the same way that the Lord Jesus Christ is praying for us: constantly.

When I think about some of the things that God has brought me through, it is almost like I have been through a desert. Picture a person in the desert crawling along, without food and water for days, bleeding and bruised. (And truly, it sometimes seemed as though my heart had bled; my heart ached, and I have been in much pain.) Now picture yourself crawling, and crawling, and crawling through the desert, not sure if you are going to make it. Just tired and wounded. Finally, you fall over and say, "Lord, one more day of this and I might become too discouraged to continue." But then you get up, and you keep going. It is a matter of perspective, and prayer will help you to have the right perspective.

If you are struggling today, and you feel like you are in a desert where no one understands and there is no fresh water, you need to pray—fall on your knees. Prayer will change things. Prayer will also change your perspective on things. Keep that in mind: Prayer will change your perspective. It is so important that as you go along, no matter how long it may take, you pray about what is happening in your household, knowing that the Spirit is also praying with you.

One of my prayers when I was first saved was from Romans 10:1: "Brethren, [with all] my heart's desire and goodwill for [Israel], I long and pray to God that they may be saved."

It was my heart's desire and prayer to God that my husband would be saved. Now I know that it was a selfish prayer. I wanted him saved because I was tired of sitting in church alone. I did not seem to fit in the congregation. There was the singles' meeting, there was the couples' retreat, and there I was—married, but without my spouse. I could not go to the couples' events. I was not really single, so I did not fit in with the singles' group. I did not want to be alone. My heart's desire was that he would be saved so that he could come and be with me, and we could go to the couples' fellowships together.

I also wanted him to be saved because I felt so challenged and threatened in our household. Everything I did was under a microscope. I kept thinking, "Once he is saved he will discover that this is not an easy walk. He will be so busy with his Christian walk that he will let me walk my walk, and he would not always be pointing an accusing finger at me." It did not dawn on me then, that I was reaping what I had sown. I wanted him saved so that he would not point out my faults as I had been pointing out his. It was my heart's desire that he would be saved, but it was for selfish reasons.

As the Lord moved in my life and helped me to mature and grow, I still prayed that same prayer, but it was with a totally different attitude and spirit. I began to see what God would be able to do in and through my husband, once he was in the kingdom. When I prayed for his salvation, it was for God's kingdom and not just for my benefit.

As you look at yourself and your spouse, look past all the things that you don't like and see what God sees. Remember, He came to save sinners; He saved us, and He can save our spouses. Ask God to help you to see all of the good in him or her. Ask yourself: What are the things that attracted you to this person? Make a list if you have to, but revisit the things that "turned you on" in the beginning. How did you end up married in the first place? Those qualities are still there. As God works in your life and helps you mature, you will be able to see how those characteristics will be a benefit to the kingdom of God. You will see how God could minister to others through your spouse. When you pray for your spouse, try to avoid the selfish prayers—the ones for your benefit. Pray earnestly, and ask God to save your mate and give you a servant's heart. Ask for a heart that serves in humility because it *has been forgiven of much.*

SUBMIT TO YOUR HUSBAND AS UNTO THE LORD

The next thing you want to do is submit to your husband as unto the Lord. *Submission* is not a bad word. The more you grow, the easier submission becomes. You are familiar with the verse: "Wives, be subject (be submissive and adapt yourselves) to your own husbands as [a service] to the Lord" (Ephesians 5:22). One of the things I like about the Amplified Bible is how it defines and clarifies the meaning. Where it says, "Wives, be subject . . ." it talks about being submissive and adapting yourself to your own husband as a service to the Lord. Part of your growth and maturity is then to learn how to serve. Christ has given us an excellent example of service. He served people; likewise, we should also serve our spouses. Marriage is really a ministry. As you grow, you will be able to serve the Lord by serving your spouse.

First Peter 3:1 says, "In like manner, you married women, be submissive to your own husbands [subordinate yourselves as being secondary to and dependent on them, and adapt yourselves to them], so that even if any do not obey the Word [of God], they may be won over not by discussion but by the [godly] lives of their wives." The act of submission creates an opportunity for you to demonstrate unconditional love. Submission is submission to position, not submission to personality.

The Word didn't say submit if your husband is saved. It says submit if you have a husband, whether he is growing spiritually or not growing at all. God does not expect us to submit, however, to anything that is unbiblical. Service and submission are two ways that you can demonstrate unconditional love. As you submit to your husband, things will begin to change. More importantly, you will begin to change.

Early in my newfound faith, whenever I came home from church, I would definitely apply the Word. I believed in applying the Word; I lived for application. I would get a verse and I would come home and do it. Noticing the change in my behavior, my husband would ask, "So, what seminar did you go to this week?" I protested, "But honey, this is the Word of the Lord. I am here to serve you; I want to submit to you." Later, I realized submission had to come from my heart because God was prompting me, not because of another workshop or seminar. What I was doing in these years was "putting on." I had zeal, but the knowledge was not there. And my husband could smell the pretense. Now, I was not pretending. I really wanted to serve José, but I was forcing the Spirit instead of yielding to Him. Big difference, huge difference, and José was razor sharp! So don't think you are fooling your spouse; he knows you and he knows genuineness. Let God do it in you.

Remember the movie *The Joy Luck Club?* One husband decided to divorce his wife because she had become so submissive that she no longer had an opinion about anything. She had also stopped being fun as a result. His wife had adopted a subservient attitude instead of the heart of a servant. She stopped interacting with him and just complied with him.

You may go home after attending a retreat or church service and really desire to change and do some things differently, and your spouse will watch to see how long the change will last. According to my husband's theory, a one-day seminar was good for a week. A weekend retreat was good for a month. So whenever I went to a seminar, he would bide the time to see how long the change would last. I had no idea he was watching until years later when he said, "Oh, yeah, I remember those seminars you went to."

I often came home fired up and applying all the principles and new techniques I would learn. Then, when I would get no response from my husband, my excitement would wane. With resignation, I would decide, "OK, what difference does it make? It will just be the same old, same old."

However, I began to realize that God required that I serve and submit to my husband as a way of life; not just because I went to a seminar, but because it was service to Him when I served my husband. This truth made it a lot easier to do it consistently. So when I passed one month, and the second month, and then the third month, in amazement my husband stopped counting. Instead, he began to expect those things.

Now, of course, that put additional pressure on me. I had established this new pattern of behavior, and he expected to see it continue. After three, four, or five good months of serving with a good attitude, serving with a gentle spirit, serving with a smile, on the first day that I grumbled his attitude was, "Hmm, I thought this was a lasting change." So I had to help educate my husband about the nature of the Christian walk.

The Christian walk does not mean that I will never stumble; it does not mean I will never sin. It means that I serve a forgiving God who is changing me, and I am growing, day by day. My constant prayer is: "Lord, please do not let me do the same things I did last year. Help me to grow from that place." When I explained that I am still growing and I have not yet arrived, it helped to ease the pressure somewhat. I reminded him that I am still human; I have not gone to heaven yet; I am not perfect. So, he was then able to say, "OK, you slipped. But, you know, I really liked it when you were doing this and this." I started to see a change in his behavior as a result of our understanding and the change in my behavior.

One thing that I must repeat, at this point, is clarification of 1 Peter 3:1. This verse says that husbands "may be won . . . by the [godly] lives of their wives." As a counselor, I have the opportunity to speak with a lot of different women who are bound, almost enslaved, to this verse, and my heart grieves. First Peter 3:1 did not say your husband would definitely get saved the day you submit. So if you are sitting under any type of doctrine that teaches that, you need to know it is a fallacy. That is not what the Word says. The Word says your husband may be won by your behavior, not that when you are Christlike he will get saved automatically.

You could not save yourselves, so a change in your behavior is not going to save anyone else. It is important that you know that; you need to free yourself if you have held that mistaken belief. Maybe you have been saved for two, three, ten years, or more, and you are still wondering what you are doing wrong. If you feel guilty about the fact that your husband or wife is not saved, remind yourself that it is God who saves. I have tried every trick in the book; so if one of those tricks really worked, my husband would have been saved years ago. But I cannot save anyone. It is by grace, through faith, that I am saved and not because of myself. So, it is important that you remember that your husband may be won over by your Christian life, but 1 Peter 3:1 is not a guarantee that he will get saved because your behavior has changed. Place your hope in God. He causes lives to change.

I don't want any of you to suffer with the burden of salvation for someone else. Now, granted, we can make intercession. We can pray for them, and we can witness to them. But even in witnessing, you don't need to witness every day, verbally, with tracts, leaving the Bible open to certain passages, etc. Your witness must be in your lifestyle. When I say walk your talk; that is your witness. A genuine authentic relationship with Christ will do this. What you do on a daily basis—how you live—that is the witness that you want to give to your spouse.

Please understand too that a witness is one who has firsthand experience. She or he simply tells what they have seen and heard—in short, what the Lord has done for them. Let your mate know the difference God has made in your life, then let it show. Or as our "foreparents" would say, "Let it shine, let it shine, let it shine!" There was another verse in that song that they improvised, which said, "Not gon' make it shine, just gon' let it shine." That's what you are after—just yielding to the Spirit.

DWELL WITH YOUR SPOUSE ACCORDING TO KNOWLEDGE

The next way that you can walk in wisdom while in an unequally yoked marital relationship is to dwell with your spouse according to knowledge. "Likewise, ye husbands, dwell with them according to knowledge, giving honour unto the wife, as unto the weaker vessel, and as being heirs together of the grace of life; that your prayers be not hindered" (1 Peter 3:7 KJV). You must know the person you are living with. You should know his or her general characteristics as a man or a woman. You should also know your mate specifically: as your husband/wife, as a friend, as a lover, and as a provider or helper. What is your spouse like as an employer? What is he or she like as an employee? Then you need to dwell with him or her according to this knowledge. You need to live considerately, acknowledging what this person is like.

This point is a fun one for me. One of the things that I must remember is that my husband is very detailed, very orderly, and very methodical. He is the "neatnik" in our household. He really believes that there is a place for everything and everything ought to be in its place. Now, for me, if it is close to its place, it is OK. I know where to find it, if it is in proximity. I have no idea how many arguments that we had because things were not in their place. About two or three years into our marriage, I asked myself one day, "Is it really that difficult to put this back? Wouldn't it make life so much easier to just put it back?" Especially since I know the man, I know how he feels about having things decent and in order. And God says, "Let all things be done decently and in order" (1 Corinthians 14:40 KJV). So if I am walking my talk and living according to the Word, it seems reasonable that I should just put it back. That is a simple example of dwelling with your spouse according to knowledge. If you know certain things about your spouse, that is to your advantage. You then need to learn how to live within those parameters. You should dwell with your spouse according to knowledge.

OBEY THE LORD IN ALL THINGS, EVEN THE DIFFICULT THINGS

Next, you want to obey the Lord in all things. Acts 5:29 says, "Then Peter and the apostles replied, We must obey God rather than men." I am frequently asked, "What if my husband asks me to do something that is unbiblical?" If your husband asks you to do something that would violate Scripture, you need to obey the Lord in all things. However, when you respond that this is not what God would have me to do, your husband needs to be able to tell that you are serious about obeying God because he has watched your life. Your refusal will seem unfair if you do whatever you want to do all the time, but when it is something he wants to do, you tell him, "God said, don't." You must be applying the Word consistently in your life. When issues arise that are questionable for you, you can then tell your husband, "I don't think God would be pleased with this action."

I can honestly say that over the years that I have been married, my husband never asked me to do anything specifically that was unbiblical. There have been some things that he asked me to do that

I just really didn't want to do. It was always an easy excuse to say, "Oh, I can't do that; I'm a Christian." But it gave the wrong image of a Christian. For years my husband thought that Christians don't have fun, Christians don't laugh, Christians don't go anywhere, Christians don't spend time with the family, they don't get together with any of their old friends, and that is not a true reflection of a Christian. He held this opinion because I gave the wrong impression. I was trying to use verses to my advantage. It is really important that as you apply the Word, you apply the Word in truth, not to your advantage.

In addition, there are some basic things that God has called us to do as Christians whether we are in unequally yoked relationships or not. God has called every Christian to fulfill the Great Commission. Acts 1:8 says, "But you shall receive power (ability, efficiency, and might) when the Holy Spirit has come upon you, and you shall be My witnesses in Jerusalem and all Judea and Samaria and to the ends (the very bounds) of the earth." Jerusalem is your witness at home. Jerusalem is where you witness to your husband and to the people in your household. However, as part of the Great Commission, God has also called you to go beyond the borders of your home.

Unfortunately, there are women who believe that as they submit to their unsaved husbands, they cannot do any other Christian service. That is not the case. The Great Commission starts in Jerusalem; so you minister in Jerusalem. Then you move out to Samaria and Judea. When the Lord ministered in Jerusalem, He did not save every soul before He left. He started the ministry, then He moved on and He came back periodically. That is the same thing you want to do in your household. Your ministry begins in the home, where you have the opportunity to minister to your husband and to grow spiritually as a result of the challenges that you may face there. But as you grow and minister at home, you then need to move out—do some things in the community, do some things in the church. You may even find yourself out in the mission field temporarily (in short-term missions, not for years). God will provide opportunities to witness for Him; but you need to remember that your boundaries extend beyond your home. There are specific things God has called you to do as a believer in Jesus Christ.

During my third year of marriage, I had the opportunity to serve as a missionary in Jamaica. I was surprised when my husband encouraged me to go. He thought it was a wonderful opportunity. He said there were a lot of people over there who did not know God, who needed to know God, who could learn a lot from me. I was wondering, "But what about you, honey? What about you?" He kept saying, "Why don't you go ahead and do that? I will manage. Everything will be OK." My husband even helped me raise the financial support I needed to go. It was just amazing to watch God work. I was able to go away for a couple of weeks and minister; but if I had not approached my husband, if I had not asked him, I would have missed that opportunity.

You will be surprised at the number of things that God will enable you to do, if you simply approach your husband and find out. Do not assume that because he is not saved you would not get a chance to do anything or that you will just have to stay at home all the time.

When your husband prefers that you would not go out and do a lot of things, you can dwell according to knowledge. Find out what you can do in your home. Is it OK to have a Bible study on a Tuesday evening? Can you host a women's prayer circle on a Saturday afternoon? Discover those things that you can do to be involved in ministry that will not negatively affect your home.

I can remember the different things that I was involved in as a new Christian. Although I was not sure at that time what the Lord was calling me to do, I had a zest and a zeal for the Lord and I wanted to serve. However, I skipped over Jerusalem, and I went straight to the uttermost parts of the earth. It is a miracle that my marriage survived. At one point, I taught toddler church, served on the usher board, sang in the choir, taught Sunday school, I was an assistant to the pastor, and worked a full-time job. There was a meeting on Monday, a meeting on Tuesday, prayer meeting on Wednesday, a choir rehearsal on Thursday, and I was never home.

I was so busy serving the church and serving the people at the church that I was not ministering at home. I often say that it was only because of the grace of God that my husband didn't leave me. As I grew in the Lord, I learned that ministry is started in Jerusalem. I was able to go back and try to start over again. Granted, I had a wise pastor who pulled me aside and said, "When are you at home? We really want you at the church; we appreciate your service, and we're glad you are excited, but maybe you should go home." At the time, I was immature, and I took it personally. I thought, "But I want to serve. I want to help. I want to make a difference." However, my pastor wisely and frankly explained, "The best difference you can make is by being at home. That is the reason your husband doesn't want to hear about the people at church. That is why he doesn't want to come here. He is fed up. You are always at church. You are always talking about what's going on with the people here and how excited you are here. Then you go home and you're miserable because your husband's not saved and there is nobody to talk to about spiritual things. You spend all of your time here serving, serving, serving."

So as you obey the Lord, it is really important that you find out what it is that you are called to do. Make sure that the Lord is really calling you to that specific area of ministry and it is not just the place where you would rather be. I didn't want to be at home. I didn't want to be under the gun. I didn't want to be watched. I wanted to be where people loved the Lord and thought that everything I did was wonderful, where the people were rejoicing and excited about the good news. I wanted to be serving, but part of my motivation for service and ministry was a desire to be free from the pressure at home.

Like me, many of you need to look at your life and ask the Lord to search your heart. Find out why you are spending so much time doing all of these other things. Is that really what you should be doing? Should you go home and spend more time ministering in Jerusalem?

Second Corinthians 2:9 says, "For this was my purpose in writing you, to test your attitude and see if you stand the test, whether you are obedient and altogether agreeable [to following my orders] in everything." It is easy to follow some orders and to pass certain tests. But if we really want to grow spiritually, we need to apply the whole Word of God to our lives. We need to lead balanced lives, which means that we are ministering in the home, as well as in the community, and in the church. But our home life should not suffer as a result of our desire to serve the Lord. And is God really pleased with our service if we are not where we ought to be?

We can serve the Lord with the praise of our lips. "Praise ye the Lord. Praise ye the name of the Lord; praise him, O ye servants of the Lord" (Psalm 135:1 KJV). "My mouth shall speak the praise of the Lord: and let all flesh bless His holy name for ever and ever" (Psalm 145:21 KJV). We do not always have to be out doing things. Your life can be a witness and a service to Him. So keep that in mind as you assess your situation. Ask the Lord to help you determine whether you should be going out in Christian service or if you should be staying home more. To walk in wisdom, you should obey the Lord in all things.

MAINTAIN THE MARRIAGE AS HONORABLE AND MAINTAIN A CLOSE RELATIONSHIP WITH THE LORD

Hebrews 13:4a says, "Let marriage be held in honor (esteemed worthy, precious, of great price, and especially dear) in all things." In an unequally yoked marriage, Christians need to be encouraged not to think divorce. Divorce should not be an option for us.

Remember, God is sovereign; God is up to something. As soon as we find ourselves thinking every time something goes wrong, "I am out of here. I do not have to put up with this," we must stop and take these thoughts captive. "[Inasmuch as we] refute arguments and theories and reasonings and every proud and lofty thing that sets itself up against the [true] knowledge of God; and we lead every thought and purpose away captive into the obedience of Christ (the Messiah, the Anointed One)" (2 Corinthians 10:5).

My mind-set is that my marriage is permanent. Even when I do not like what is going on in my household, I know we are going to make it through. I encourage myself with God's Word. Scripture tells me that this too shall pass. "Weeping may endure for a night, but joy comes in the morning" (Psalm 30:5b). As I acknowledge and obey the Lord, I am expecting God to show up and do something. I don't know what He is going to do. I don't know how He is going to fix it or how He is going to change it. But I know that He is God, and I know He is able. I know that He desires to work things out for my good.

It is vitally important in your Christian walk that you maintain a close relationship with the Lord, especially if you are in an unbalanced relationship. John 14:16 says, "I will ask the Father, and He will give you another Comforter (Counselor, Helper, Intercessor, Advocate, Strengthener, and Standby), that He may remain with you forever." As we maintain a close relationship with the Lord, we realize that we have an Advocate with the Father. We have someone who is standing close by. We have a Counselor, a Comforter, someone who is very well aware of our situations and the things that we are dealing with. We have someone who is a Standby for us, who can help us to grow spiritually and help us to mature in Christ, no matter what the circumstances.

John 15:4 says, "Dwell in Me, and I will dwell in you. [Live in Me, and I will live in you.] Just as no branch can bear fruit of itself without abiding in (being vitally united to) the vine, neither can you bear fruit unless you abide in Me." It is easy to do things on a day-to-day basis and not realize when you are straying from the Spirit. Unless you are spending time in the Word, you cannot know what God requires of you. As you study the Word and spend time with Him, it will become clear how God wants you to walk. John 15:7 says, "If you live in Me [abide vitally united to Me] and My words remain in you and continue to live in your hearts, ask whatever you will, and it shall be done for you."

Abide in Christ

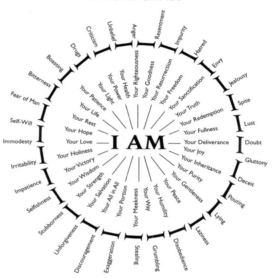

Figure 3-1

This diagram will help you as you live the Christian life. It will show you when you are abiding in the Lord and when you are walking in the flesh. Look in the center of the circle where it says "I am." This is the position that knowing the great I AM, our Counselor, our Father, our God, must have in our lives. He is our light, hope, strength, deliverance, fullness, truth, resurrection, meekness, and humility. He is all of the good things that we are. When we are focused on the outside of the circle: when there is doubt or unbelief, when we find ourselves pouting when things did not go our way, when we are exaggerating how bad the situation is, when we are selfish or want our spouses saved for self-centered reasons, when there is a lot of self-will or bitterness, we know that we are then walking in the flesh (doing what we want to do regardless of what the Word has to say). We need to come and submit ourselves to the Lord, bow before Him, ask forgiveness, and then go on.

As you live in an unbalanced relationship, know that God requires that you grow. You will have to give an account for every action, attitude, and thought. Therefore, it is critically important that you do what is pleasing to Him—that you do not jeopardize your marriage or use your spouse as an excuse for not growing spiritually. We must apply wisdom.

In summary, to walk in wisdom we need to walk our talk, intercede for our spouses and our marriages, submit to our husbands as unto the Lord, dwell with our spouses according to knowledge, obey the Lord in all things, and maintain our marriages as honorable and maintain a close relationship with the Lord. "For to the person who pleases Him God gives wisdom and knowledge and joy" (Ecclesiastes 2:26a).

Let's pray.

> *Heavenly Father, You know our hearts and our challenges. I thank You for Your Word. In it, we find hope and encouragement. As we apply it, we are edified and lifted up so we can then move forward and grow as You would have us to grow.*
>
> *Dear Lord, I thank You that You hear us when we pray. Whenever our hearts are heavy, we can cry out to You, Lord. We can simply groan about those things that only You can understand. Father, we cry for help. Lord, it is a difficult walk, but we know that You do not give us more than we can bear. We thank You for giving us*

Your wisdom, power, and comfort.

Father, we thank You for the opportunity we have to witness to our spouses and live before them as an example of the change that Christ makes in the life of a believer. We pray that our spouses would be saved— that they would come to know You, live to serve You, and make a difference for the kingdom. These things we pray in Your Son Jesus' name. Amen.

Prayer request

For David - Terry's husband - friends have been coming but David won't.

Nancy & John mullins
Tara got Job = Praise

Cheri & dog + Family
Mathew = Tina's Son

Buy House = Chris - Hope for they would enjoy

CHAPTER FOUR

Maximizing Your Marriage

Each of our marriages has a visible and an invisible story line. Both of these stories are lived simultaneously, but usually only one is told. Our lives are like an ever-changing drama. Some of it is horror. Some of it is comedy. Some of it is a love story. Whatever the story line, it's good to know that God is the director of the invisible (and the entire) story. He is the "author and the finisher of our faith" (Hebrews 12:2 KJV). We must allow Him to direct our steps and then follow His instructions. He has written the script and all we have to do is live out our part. Certainly, God is the star, and we are privileged to have a role in His production. God has designed a part for each of us. The question is: How well will you play your part?

In the movies, certain characters merely stroll by and never say a word; they have a walk-on part. Some characters say just one line of dialog in an entire two-hour-long movie, and they get paid for that. If we would just walk the Christian walk, then we could carry out our part, no matter how big or how small. If we could just get our lines right, we would get paid in heaven; there is a reward for that. "But I say unto you, That every idle word that men shall speak, they shall give account thereof in the day of judgment. For by thy words thou shalt be justified, and by thy words thou shalt be condemned" (Matthew 12:36–37 KJV). Too often, we have an opportunity to say one line, and we blow it. We say the wrong thing, maybe something sarcastic, and then we end up falling before the Lord asking for forgiveness and needing to humble ourselves before our spouse to ask his or her forgiveness. All because of that one line. One line can ruin an entire scene. So think about how you are playing out your role in your marriage. What are your one-liners? What are your walk-on parts?

OUR ROLE IN MARRIAGE

As Christians, we must be very careful about the part we play in our marriages. When you get a walk-on part, be sure to walk the Christian walk. When you have an opportunity to speak (and that should not be all day long every day), make sure that what you say is wise. Scripture tells us that a foolish woman tears down her house. "Every wise woman buildeth her house: but the foolish plucketh it down with her hands" (Proverbs 14:1 KJV). You want to build your house. You can influence your story by what you do and say. Being aware of your role in life can help you do this.

We really need to rely on the Spirit, His wisdom, and His discernment to discover how we should approach our spouse. A lot of what we say is unnecessary. When we get those opportunities for one-liners, we need to make sure it is something that is edifying, something that is pleasing, something that is encouraging, something that will build up and not tear down your spouse or your relationship.

We must also avoid the temptation to try to carry out somebody else's part or try to act the way somebody else is acting. Have you ever watched a show where somebody was doing an imitation and it was a bad imitation? That is how a lot of us are sometimes. We try to imitate what somebody else is doing and what we thought was working, when, in fact, we have no idea what is going on when they close the door.

When you are in an unequally yoked relationship, one of the things that can really trip you up is looking at *other people's marriages*. It is so easy to look at other couples and think, "I wish my spouse was a Christian and my relationship was like theirs." Do not set yourself up to stumble. Do not look to the left or to the right; look up from whence cometh your help. Look up! Your help comes from the Lord. "I will lift up mine eyes unto the hills, from whence cometh my help. My help cometh from the Lord, which made heaven and earth" (Psalm 121:1–2 KJV). Remember, if you look to the Lord and learn to praise Him for your spouse regardless of what is going on around you, you will have that abundant joy that He desires for you.

FIVE TYPES OF MARRIAGES

As I've considered the different phases of my own marriage and those of the women I have counseled, the following five types of marriages have been identified. Alliteration often makes things easier to remember, so these titles all contain the letter "M."

- *Murderous and Maligned*
- *The Memories and the Mask*
- *Mutual Mediocrity and Mellow*
- *Magnetic and Motivated*
- *Marvelous, Model, and Maximized*

The unfortunate thing about many unequally yoked marital relationships is that they are methodical. Marriage partners can fall into a routine, even when they know it is not a good situation. Too often, the relationship becomes like a tragic melodrama and the couple resign themselves to endure to the end. As you read about these five types of marriages, consider the similarities in your own marital relationship.

Murderous and Maligned

Some people stay in Murderous and Maligned marriages where they live day by day not knowing if they are going to make it through. This type of marriage relationship is filled with conflict—arguments, hassles, accusations, and fights (sometimes even violence) that constantly occur over the simplest of things. These marriages are marked by personal and relational pain. You can sense a hostile environment as soon as you walk through the door. People in this type of relationship often don't even want to go home at the end of the day because they don't know what they are going to walk into.

Shortly after I was saved, my marriage fell into this category. It didn't have to be that way, but I was so pious and self-righteous. I knew the Lord, and I had changed my lifestyle. I thought I was living perfectly upright. Not! I took advantage of every opportunity to point out my husband's sins, his shortcomings, and all of his faults. My life was the only light in the house and it was not shining the best reflection of Christ, and it caused major conflict.

It seemed that my husband wanted to debate about everything. But I did not know enough to debate; I did not even know enough Scripture to argue. Although I knew in whom I believed, I could not explain why. I wanted to be able to stand my ground. Scripture does say to be ready to give an account for the hope that is within you. "But sanctify the Lord God in your hearts: and be ready always to give an answer to every man that asketh you a reason of the hope that is in you with meekness and fear" (1 Peter 3:15 KJV). However, it does not say that we should argue about it or beat people over the head with the Bible, but be ready to give an account. I was so frustrated, and I couldn't understand why he didn't love the Lord. Especially since he could quote all the right Bible verses. Why didn't he want to sit in heavenly places? I mean, that's what I was doing, or so I thought. Why didn't he want to be set free from sin and empowered by the Holy Spirit? In retrospect, I guess I was no motivation for him.

We went back and forth during our second year of marriage. When my husband encouraged me to go to church, I was almost afraid to go because as soon as I came home, he would ask: "So what did the pastor talk about today?" I kept thinking, "Please don't ask me." When I gave him the sermon notes, he would read them over and say, "Oh. So this is what they are teaching you at that church over there." I thought, "Why do we always have to debate about this?" And the service would be so wonderful, sometimes I would just ride around the block before coming home, while I wondered, "OK, what am I going to walk into this time?"

The Memories and the Mask

For couples who live in marriages made up of "The Memories and the Mask," the relationship has become merely an empty shell. They are not moving forward and nothing seems to be going right; but they still have faint memories of what it used to be, and they live out the pretense that it still is. Some of you may be in this type of situation. You may be able to look back to a point when life was good, or at least tolerable, and when things were not always in conflict. Let's stay there awhile. Yeah, those were the best days of our lives. We were so in love and there was nothing too good for us. Yeah, the love song that we claimed as "our song" still bring sweet memories and we beam with the joy of yesterday's love. You can survive and get there again.

My husband and I survived this stage, too. Imagine going from a first year of candlelight dinners, an immaculate house, and having your bath drawn in the evenings to sitting in the bathroom on the floor crying and thinking about what married life used to be like. At this point in our marriage, I could not live in the present, and I could not pray about the future. I was too busy being stuck in the past. I would sit in the room and just stare at the walls and think, "Man, I remember when things were good. Wow, I remember when we used to laugh and talk all of the time and go places." I had all of these memories of how good life used to be.

Then there is the mask—the need to present the appearance that everything is fine. I needed the mask because people remembered that first year of marriage. They remembered me telling them how great life was. So whenever I left the house, it was almost like I had to stop and get dressed mentally. I would put on the mask and go out: "Hi! I am happy! Life is wonderful! I love my husband and he loves me and we have a wonderful marriage. Everything is great at home!" But I would be crying behind the mask: "Please do not ask me how I am because I am dying on the inside. And don't touch me because I will surely burst into tears. Just let me hold back the tears until I can get back in the house and allow the drama to continue."

Inside I longed for someone to say, "Sabrina, are you OK?" and then allow me to pour out my heart; to actually listen and allow me to say, "I am really struggling, but I know the Lord is able; He will sustain me. It is a day-to-day challenge but He has empowered me to go on." But I could not remove my mask because I had built this image that life was wonderful. I could not stop and tell people that I was catching it at home, or that marriage was difficult and the man was driving me crazy (and I him).

When people see you at church, on your job, or in the community, they have no idea of the pain you may live with. They have no idea of the situation you may have left at home. Most of us walk into church bouncing and laughing and smiling, enjoying the fellowship; and everyone just assumes that life is wonderful and that we have a handle on things. But we can be smiling on the outside and on the inside just dying—almost literally falling apart—waiting for someone to stop and stand still long enough to hear an honest response when they ask the question, "How are you?" Sadly, our tendency, even as Christians, is to ask someone how they are doing, and before that person can answer, we are gone and we are asking someone else how they are doing.

I was not doing well and I really needed help. I knew that I loved him, and I knew that we could get past this. But, my constant prayer was, "Lord, when? When will we ever get past this?"

The change did not happen overnight. Church was my sanctuary, and it sometimes seemed like I had held almost every position in the church. I wanted to be anyplace but home. So I looked for a reason to have to go to the church.

But my pastor sent me home. I thought, "Oh, I'm suffering for Jesus. I will be a martyr. I'm suffering; I'm suffering." And I kept wondering, "Why would he send me home?" But at home, I learned that you don't have to be at the church every day to have a relationship with the Lord. Your relationship really does start at home; it starts in your heart. I learned to quit praying for myself, to quit moaning about my situation, waiting on my change to come, and instead to spend the time on my knees for my husband, for my marriage.

Some of you may know how difficult it is to wait for a change to come. Yes, it will come, but in God's own timing according to His plan. God is always on time. When I quit asking "When?" and "Why?" and quit trying to change my situation, and I asked God to change me—then things changed. God changed my heart, my approach, and my response to my marriage.

Later, when I could see improvement in our relationship, I was happy that I had gone in for counseling, but it took me a while to come to that place. I wore the mask for a while and I held on to all of the old memories. The Memories and the Mask devitalized relationship lasted about three or four years. I was stuck for a long time. But God used this time to teach me more about His ways, and then I moved forward.

Mutual Mediocrity and Mellow

In a Mutual Mediocrity and Mellow marriage, the partners live parallel lives and are usually friendly. They have worked out a relationship in which there is typically more separateness than togetherness. The quality of the marriage is based on stability. When neither partner is working to improve the relationship, the marriage becomes stagnant. The couple will often resign themselves to mediocrity.

After living in a Murderous and Maligned relationship for about a year and in The Memories and the Mask (longing for the good old days) for three or four years, my husband and I came to accept each other's differences. We had developed a Mutual Mediocrity and Mellow relationship. We both had separate activities, goals, and interests. I did my thing and he did his thing, and if our things happened to meet—great.

We got together, took out our calendars and date books, and checked our schedules. Then we planned a date when we both were in town. "I am going to a conference here. Are you going to be home on the weekend?" "I am in town." "Great, let's get together for a date." "What do you have coming up next week? Can you come with me to this?" "Well, you know you have to do a church function because I did a fraternity function." "OK. I will write that down." We came to a place in our relationship where we kind of went along on parallel tracks, but we weren't really working together toward a mutual relationship, goal, purpose, or vision.

Magnetic and Motivated

The Magnetic and Motivated marriage relationship is characterized by frequent interaction and communication, interspersed with times of separateness. The partners are intimate but individuals. They each consider the other to be their very best friend.

Once, when preparing to speak at an upcoming women's conference, I had all kinds of books lying around. My old tendency had been to leave Christian tracts, books, and notes for my husband all over the house, in his lunch bag, and in his pockets. So when he saw the book, he assumed I had left it out for him. Although this was no longer my pattern, he still remembered what I used to do.

After a few books had been missing for about a week, I asked, "Honey, have you seen my books anywhere?" He said, "Oh, they are in my locker at work." I said, "Give me my books; what are they doing in your locker?" He explained, "I thought you wanted me to read them."

When he came home, he said, "Well, I finished the books. They were enlightening." I cautiously answered, "OK." Then he asked, "So, where do you think we are? How would you describe our marriage?" I thought, "Hmm, do I really have to answer?" But I said, "You know, we both have separate interests. We are friendly, there is no fire, and we are not attacking each other. We have learned to live with each other. So I would say Mutual Mediocrity because we are mellow and everything is OK."

But my husband objected, "No, no. We are Magnetic and Motivated." He explained, "Mutual Mediocrity described our relationship a long time ago, but we are walking together now." I thought aloud, "Are we? Oh, this is exciting; I can't wait to go tell everybody. Are we really growing here?"

As I began to think about our relationship, I realized that we had been spending a lot of time together lately. The Lord had really convicted me about some of the changes I needed to make, and I had been earnestly trying to make them. Then I decided to look back through the book to see exactly what he had based his opinion on. When I looked again I thought, "Maybe we are kind of vitalized." For the last five or six months, we had spent more time laughing and talking. I thought, "OK, that is key for being Magnetic: we communicate. We talk with each other, not at each other. We talk about things that are relevant as opposed to just the weather and the news." We were beginning to work together in the relationship.

My husband's view of the marriage and the actual changes took me by surprise. I was so busy working on my part of the relationship that I did not notice our growth as a couple. It was exciting to know that my husband felt like we were Magnetic and Motivated. I was not even looking for this. I thought, "Oh, this is good, Lord. Wow, this is progress! It has been nine years, but it is progress." Then I thought, "Hey, maybe one day we really will be Maximized!" And I prayed, "Father, make his heart ready to receive Your Word."

After that discussion, every time my husband read one of my books, he would wait about a week or two, then come back to discuss it with me. He would say things like, "What about that book on your shelf? Didn't it say that wives should do this, this, and this?" Sometimes I would have to say, "What shelf are you on—let me look at that one." We were having a great time laughing and studying about marriage. The challenges we posed to each other weren't cynical; instead they encouraged us to rise to the occasion for intimate interaction.

I have often thought to myself, "This is a real blessing, this ministry the Lord has given me in my marriage, even through all of my difficult times. With all of the books and resources I have collected, my husband is now able to go into our library and read those books. That he would even have an interest in picking up a religious book is a miracle!"

Scripture says the Word will not return void. "So shall my word be that goeth forth out of my mouth: it shall not return unto me void, but it shall accomplish that which I please, and it shall prosper in the thing whereto I sent it" (Isaiah 55:11 KJV). I prayed that it would fall on good ground and make a difference in his life, and it has. But in the process, I have learned so much. God has a way of dealing with us. Many times when we are trying to present something to someone else, He will teach us that lesson first, so we can have empathy with the situation of others, not just sympathy.

Marvelous, Model, and Maximized

The Marvelous, Model, and Maximized marriage operates according to God's design. The partners in this type of marriage are very close. The two have become one flesh. Their lives are intermixed and interwoven, and their goals are virtually interchangeable.

After seventeen years of marriage, we are finally heading toward this marvelous place in our relationship. I am looking toward the day when we will have the total marriage that God desires for us. My husband has come to know the Lord—not just know about Him but know Him in a personal relationship. He has come to the place where he desires to live for God, not only when it is convenient, but as a lifestyle. To maximize our marriage relationship will require growth in our love, and commitment to God and to each other. Our goal is to become a marvelous model for the body of Christ.

Ephesians 5:21–32: *Submitting yourselves one to another in the fear of God. Wives, submit yourselves unto your own husbands, as unto the Lord. For the husband is the head of the wife, even as Christ is the head of the church: and he is the saviour of the body. Therefore as the church is subject unto Christ, so let the wives be to their own husbands in every thing. Husbands, love your wives, even as Christ also loved the church, and gave himself for it; that he might sanctify and cleanse it with the washing of water by the word, that he might present it to himself a glorious church, not having spot, or wrinkle, or any such thing; but that it should be holy and without blemish. So ought men to love their wives as their own bodies. He that loveth his wife loveth himself. For no man ever yet hated his own flesh; but nourisheth and cherisheth it, even as the Lord the church: For we are members of his body, of his flesh, and of his bones. For this cause shall a man leave his father and mother, and shall be joined unto his wife, and they two shall be one flesh. This is a great mystery: but I speak concerning Christ and the church."* (KJV)

I know that this will only happen as we grow in the Lord and work together (in one accord) with Him, realizing the Marvelous, Model, and Maximized marriage is a process. In the meantime, we must do everything possible to work toward this goal.

YOUR MARRIAGE RELATIONSHIP

Now that you have looked at these five types of marriages, take time to consider your story and the role that God would have you to play. Remember, you do not have to be stuck where you are. It is God's power, active and available in and through you, that will enable you to move from one place to the next.

You can move forward—even when you feel like your marriage is maximized and you have the best of the best. God's Word says that we will not be complete until the day that Jesus returns. "Being confident of this very thing, that he which hath begun a good work in you will perform it until the day of Jesus Christ" (Philippians 1:6a KJV). So there is progress to be made and more for you to attain. There are still some steps that you can take and some things that you can work on.

STEPS TO MAXIMIZING YOUR MARRIAGE

It takes "P-O-W-E-R" to maximize your marriage.

Praise and prayer

Obedience to God

Witness His works

Endure to the end

Reflect and rejoice

Step 1: Praise and Prayer

The first step to maximizing your marriage is to give God *praise* and spend time with Him in *prayer*. Scripture has much to say about praise. Here are a few verses:

"Rejoice in the Lord, O you [uncompromisingly] righteous [you upright in right standing with God]; for praise is becoming and appropriate for those who are upright [in heart]" (Psalm 33:1 AMPLIFIED). You need to praise God on a continual basis. Praise has nothing to do with your situation. It has to do with the goodness of God. God is good all of the time; and all of the time God is good. That is not a question and answer, it is a statement of fact. No matter what you may face in life, remember that God is good; so praise is always in order.

"'Blessed is she who has believed that what the Lord has said to her will be accomplished!' And Mary said: 'My soul glorifies the Lord and my spirit rejoices in God my Savior'" (Luke 1:45–47 NIV). This should be our response as well. The Bible is filled with promises to those who believe that what the Lord has said will be accomplished in their lives. If you have come to know and believe the Lord, just the joy of your salvation should cause you to have a spirit of praise.

"Bless the Lord, O my soul: and all that is within me, bless his holy name. Bless the Lord, O my soul, and forget not all his benefits" (Psalm 103:1–2 KJV). Make a praise list. Start by praising the Lord that you woke up. Praise the Lord that you can write a list.

Praise the Lord that you can see the list. Then praise the Lord you can think straight and know what to write. There are so many reasons to praise God. Praise Him for His majesty, His works, and all of His attributes. Praise God for your spouse, your children, and your household. Praise Him for any number of things: for the sunshine and the stars, for the grass and the breeze, for health, life, and breath itself. Each day write down some of the things that you can praise God for. Include thanks and praise for prayers that He has answered so that you never forget His goodness.

"Man that is born of a woman is of few days, and full of trouble" (Job 14:1 KJV). You need a praise list because things are bound to go wrong. If you know that, don't be upset when stuff happens. Expect trials and tribulations, but don't let the trials and tribulations control your outlook. When things go wrong, review your praise list and answered prayers to remind yourself of all the blessings you can be excited about.

"Let my mouth be filled with thy praise and with thy honour all the day" (Psalm 71:8 KJV). You cannot praise God and curse God (or anyone else) at the same time. As Christians, our mouths should be filled with praise and our spirits should be overflowing with praise. A spirit of praise helps us to focus on God and avoid grumbling and murmuring and complaining. We don't want to be like the children of Israel, always complaining about one thing after another as though nothing is ever good enough. We can forget about all of the circumstances that aren't going our way and begin to thank God for who Jesus is and for what He has done in our lives.

"Enter into his gates with thanksgiving, and into his courts with praise: be thankful unto him, and bless his name" (Psalm 100:4 KJV). A thankful heart will help us stop thinking about all of the things that aren't right, all of the things we would like to change, and all of the "what ifs." God does not waste a moment. Everything that happens occurs for a reason. Even when we can't make any sense out of it, we know that God's ways and His thoughts are much higher than ours. "For as the heavens are higher than the earth, so are my ways higher than your ways, and my thoughts than your thoughts" (Isaiah 55:9 KJV). We do not have to understand everything. Our job is to have faith in God. And our pursuit is to know Him as intimately as we possibly can and then to become more and more like Him.

"Why are you cast down, O my inner self? And why should you moan over me and be disquieted within me? Hope in God and wait expectantly for Him, for I shall yet praise Him, my Help and my God" (Psalm 42:5 AMPLIFIED). Like David, begin to encourage yourself. Remember that God is your hope and your help. Expect that God will do good things. Knowing that God desires the best for you should make you excited. Anything less than the best is not what He wants; this truth alone should cause you to praise the Lord.

"But I say unto you, Love your enemies, bless them that curse you, do good to them that hate you, and pray for them which despitefully use you, and persecute you" (Matthew 5:44 KJV). Next, make a prayer list, if you do not already have one. Be sure that your list includes more than just you and the things that concern you. We should be praying for all of those around us, especially those who we feel are despitefully using us. Even in unfair or difficult situations, we are not to render evil for evil; instead we are commanded to do good. "See that none render evil for evil unto any man; but ever follow that which is good, both among yourselves, and to all men" (1 Thessalonians 5:15 KJV).

During my second year of marriage, I had a hard time praying for anybody except myself. But now when facing marital problems or struggles, I realize that my husband is also struggling and I pray for him. I pray for his day on the job and the people he has to interact with. I pray for safe travel home and his attitude when he comes in the door. I pray for our conversation, and I pray that I will be able to understand his perspective and concerns.

Similarly, you want to learn to pray for your spouse and to pray for his situation. Don't just pray for yourself or that God would bring about a change and that your change would come. Your change may not come for many years. You do not know how long you are going to have to wait. Instead, in prayer or in praise, invite God to work out His will. Also remember that God desires to work some things in and through you. So make a praise list and a prayer list. Continually praise God and constantly be in prayer.

Step 2: Obedience to God

The second step in maximizing your marriage is to obey the Lord.

"And Pharaoh said, Who is the Lord, that I should obey his voice to let Israel go? I know not the Lord, neither will I let Israel go" (Exodus 5:2 KJV). If you know who God is, you need to do what God says. You do not want to be guilty of pride and disobedience like Pharaoh or suffer the consequences of refusing to obey God's voice. You should honor and obey the Lord your God.

"But this thing commanded I them, saying, Obey my voice, and I will be your God, and ye shall be my people: and walk ye in all the ways that I have commanded you, that it may be well unto you" (Jeremiah 7:23 KJV). We want things to go well in our life and in our marriages. God's desire is not to limit our freedom or take away our fun. God wants the best for our lives. Obedience to God brings blessing.

"Wives, submit yourselves unto your own husbands, as unto the Lord" (Ephesians 5:22 KJV). God's Word says that we are to submit to our husbands, as it is fitting in the Lord. Many women in unequally yoked marriages have a hard time with submission. However, the type of submission that God commands is a good thing. It is for our protection; it provides a covering for us. Scripture also says, "We ought to obey God rather than men" (Acts 5:29b KJV). Clearly, in submitting to our husbands, we are not to disobey God.

"Behold, to obey is better than sacrifice" (1 Samuel 15:22b KJV).

Obedience is always better than sacrifice. Do not try to make deals with God. Don't go to church and pay penance for all the things you have or have not done. Just obey the Lord.

"Thy word is a lamp unto my feet, and a light unto my path" (Psalm 119:105 KJV). It is the Lord Jesus Christ that we must follow. He has laid a path of righteousness for us, and we need to walk in it. As we study God's Word and obey it, we will understand the way that God would have us to walk.

"Call to Me and I will answer you and show you great and mighty things, fenced in and hidden, which you do not know (do not distinguish and recognize, have knowledge of and understand)" (Jeremiah 33:3 AMPLIFIED). In addition to studying God's Word, we need to be quiet and listen to God in prayer. We cannot hear the voice of the Lord if we are the only one doing the talking, always telling Him what we want from Him—always asking for things. At some point in prayer, we need to just fall on our face before the Lord and listen with an open heart to what He has to say. Part of prayer is asking, "Lord, what would You have me to do? How would You have me respond?" Be still and wait for an answer so that you can be obedient to Him.

Step 3: Witness His Works

The third step in maximizing your marriage is to witness His works.

"O taste and see that the Lord is good: blessed is the man that trusteth in him" (Psalm 34:8 KJV). We need to watch for God. The Lord is constantly saying, "Look and see; taste and see; witness My works." God is always doing a new thing right in our midst. Too often, we are focused only on our situations or feelings, and we overlook the blessings of God.

"The humble shall see this, and be glad: and your heart shall live that seek God" (Psalm 69:32 KJV). All around you miracles take place. Do not miss them. Witness the power of God active and available in your life. God has not stopped working because your husband or wife is not saved. He has not removed Himself from your situation. You need to witness His work and see what He is doing.

"Look at the nations and watch—and be utterly amazed. For I am going to do something in your days that you would not believe, even if you were told" (Habakkuk 1:5 NIV). One of my favorite books is Habakkuk. Habakkuk was a prophet who knew God. But, in chapter 1, he complained and questioned God about things that seemed unjust. In other words, he was "going off": "God, where are You? What are You doing? What are You up to? Why are You allowing this? Don't You see what is going on with me?" And the Lord responded and said, "Watch and see. I am going to do something big."

Many of us would not have believed what God was going to do even if we had been told. In fact, when I think of the number of women I encourage, teach, or counsel who are in unequally yoked relationships, I know I would not have believed it. I can recall when I first went in to see my pastor for counseling. He said, "Sabrina, at some point you will have a ministry for women who are in your same situation." I couldn't imagine that anyone else's situation was even similar to mine. It seemed hopeless. I was still committed to my marriage, and the vows I had taken "until death do us part." But it was hard to believe that we were going to make it through, and harder to believe that something good was going to come of it. Although I was told, I could not believe it.

"But blessed are your eyes, for they see: and your ears, for they hear" (Matthew 13:16 KJV). You should be watching for God's glory right there in your household. Some days it's a miracle that I control my tongue. It's the grace of God that I do not say all of the things that I could say, that I want to say, or that I think about saying. That is a miracle. It is a miracle that my husband kept me. It's easy to think about how I stayed married to him; but he stayed married to me, too, and sometimes I am not easy to live with. When I stop to think about things like that, I know that is a miracle.

"But as for me, I watch in hope for the LORD; I wait for God my Savior; my God will hear me" (Micah 7:7 NIV). Look for God to show up. Watch for His presence and wait for His power to work things out. Do not miss Him. Focus on God and witness His works.

Step 4: Endure to the End

The fourth step in maximizing your marriage is to endure to the end.

"What therefore God hath joined together, let not man put asunder" (Matthew 19:6b KJV). Marriage was designed to be until death do you part. However, over half of the marriages today end in divorce. People are taking the easy way out. That's unfortunate; it is not God's design. The Word of God clearly says that what God has joined together, let no man (or woman) put asunder.

As Christians, we must be encouraged not to think divorce. Divorce should not be an option for us. As soon as we start thinking, every time something goes wrong, "I am out of here—I do not have to put up with this," we invite strife, depression, bitterness, and anger into the marriage relationship.

I believe in the institution of marriage. I believe in the holy estate before the Lord. My mind-set is that marriage is permanent. I purposed in my heart the day I married my husband that we were together until death do us part. The first time we had a problem, divorce didn't cross my mind. Even when I didn't like what was going on in my household, I knew we were going to make it. Through my relationship with Christ and study of the Word, God had given me hope. I had a confident expectation that my husband and I would one day rejoice in our relationship. Even though I couldn't see it, Scripture tells me that this too shall pass. "Weeping may endure for a night, but joy comes in the morning" (Psalm 30:5 paraphrased). So I am always expecting God to show up and do something. I don't know what He is going to do. I don't know how He is going to fix it. I don't know how He is going to change it. But I know that He is God, and I know He can. I know that He desires to do so.

"Let us not become weary in doing good, for at the proper time we will reap a harvest if we do not give up" (Galatians 6:9 NIV). As Christians, we must be determined to endure; we can't be ready to give up just because everything seems to go wrong. This is a result of our narrow view; we do not see God's bigger picture. We must decide to endure to the end. That one decision has helped me so much. I do not feel like I'm going to give up at any point. It enables me to pray with bold determination, "No matter what it is, Lord, I am going to work this thing through. I am going to get into Your Word and draw closer to You and find out what it is that You want me to do in this particular situation." My commitment is to endure to the end. I am not planning to give up any time soon.

"'Why then,' they asked, 'did Moses command that a man give his wife a certificate of divorce and send her away?' Jesus replied, 'Moses permitted you to divorce your wives because your hearts were hard. But it was not this way from the beginning'" (Matthew 19:7–8 NIV). Jesus explained that divorce was allowed because of the hardness of man's heart, not because it was God's will. In Scripture, there are a couple of clauses in which divorce is permitted. People tend to point to these passages and say, "What about in situations of adultery? What about this, or what about that?"

However, we should also remember that even while He hung on the cross, our Lord prayed, "Father, forgive them; for they know not what they do" (Luke 23:34 KJV). Choosing to forgive is never easy. And there is a lot involved in offering forgiveness after adultery. You have to reestablish trust, reestablish the relationship, and then there is a rebuilding process that must take place. But with God's help, it can be done.

"Love suffers long and is kind. It bears all things, believes all things, hopes all things, endures all things. Love never fails" (1 Corinthians 13:4a, 7–8a paraphrased). We must remember from whence we have come. God loved us while we were yet sinners, and we need to ask for God's help to love our spouse beyond his/her faults and in spite of the things that he/she does wrong. We must pray that God will give us the kind of love that never fails. The love of God allows us to forgive our mate—even of adultery.

"Endure hardship with us like a good soldier of Christ Jesus. No one serving as a soldier gets involved in civilian affairs—he wants to please his commanding officer" (2 Timothy 2:3–4 NIV). Our Christian walk is equated to being a soldier in an army. Scripture talks about persevering through hard times, enduring hardship like a soldier. When you are in an army, you fight. You are not there on a picnic. You must be girded up. You are supposed to be in full armor, prepared to fight, ready for the battle, and willing to take out a few folks, if need be. You are supposed to be enduring as a good soldier. So be ready to endure and forgive your spouse's transgressions.

Do not expect things to lighten up just because you went to counseling or just because you have read a few verses. You have an adversary in this battle and it is Satan, not your spouse. The adversary will intensify his attacks when he sees that his schemes no longer work. He's going to come at you from another angle. He has been knocking you upside your head with the same old thing, week after week. But when you get a handle on that, he will start doing something different. He is going to come another way. Do not be surprised. During the time when things seem to be going well, rejoice and thank God. But know that the enemy is coming back. He has not given up. He's going to be hassling you until the very end. But you just fight the good fight.

"When you pass through the waters, I will be with you; and when you pass through the rivers, they will not sweep over you. When you walk through the fire, you will not be burned; the flames will not set you ablaze" (Isaiah 43:2 NIV). Remember that you are not alone. Whenever you endeavor to please God and make a commitment to the Lord to endure to the end, no matter what comes, God's Word says that He will go with you through the fire and the floods. God will be right there with you.

"And let us run with patience the race that is set before us, looking unto Jesus the author and finisher of our faith" (Hebrews 12:1b–2a KJV). So, do not just take the easy way out; plan to endure to the end. In the race that God has set for you, the role that He intends for you to play, don't walk off the stage (or get off course) before the play (race) is over. Stay to the end; wait to see how things unfold. God has given us His Word and His strength. Trust God and endure to the end.

"For the revelation awaits an appointed time; it speaks of the end and will not prove false. Though it linger, wait for it; it will certainly come and will not delay" (Habakkuk 2:3 NIV). Habakkuk tells us, though the revelation lingers, wait for it, because it will come at the appointed time. Believe that there's an appointed time for your spouse to get saved, that there's an appointed time for your marriage to be growing and nurturing, and that there's an appointed time for you to give a testimony about God's goodness. There is an appointed time, so wait for God.

Step 5: Reflect and Rejoice

The fifth step in maximizing your marriage is to reflect and rejoice.

"Many, O LORD my God, are the wonders you have done. The things you planned for us no one can recount to you; were I to speak and tell of them, they would be too many to declare" (Psalm 40:5 NIV). The Lord has done wonderful things. Know that God is up to something, and He wants to use you as His instrument, a tool in part of His work. That is such an awesome, awesome place to be. Learn to reflect and rejoice. Remember all of the good things that God has done. Just remembering the goodness of God is cause to rejoice.

In Scripture, the children of Israel were constantly being told to remember—remember God's goodness, remember His faithfulness (Exodus 13:3; 20:8; 32:13; Numbers 15:39-40; Deuteronomy 5:15; 8:2, 18; 9:7; 15:15; 16:3, 12; 24:18). Over and over again, we read Moses' admonition not to forget (Deuteronomy 4:23; 6:12; 8:11, 14, 19; 9:7; 25:19). Do not forget the goodness of God; do not forget the salvation of God; do not forget the deliverance of God.

Like the Israelites, we must take time to reflect and remember. Remember the goodness of God in your marriage and your situation. Think about the times that God has shown up. God is still providing "manna from heaven" today. God is still "parting the Red Sea" in seemingly hopeless situations. So, what are your Red Sea experiences? When has the Lord made a way for you? When has He rained manna from heaven to supernaturally provide for you? Remember the Passover? Were there times in your life when the Lord passed over your household and blessed you? Those are the things you want to reflect on and rejoice about. Those are the things you want to remember.

Forget the bad times, but remember the things that God teaches you through them. If you are on the other side of it, God has brought you through, and you should have learned some things. The things that you learn along the way are also things to remember. As you go through and overcome trying times, ask yourself: What is God trying to teach me? What characteristic is He building in my life? What fruit of the Spirit is He developing?

"And we know that in all things God works for the good of those who love him, who have been called according to his purpose" (Romans 8:28 NIV). Sometimes, we look at a particular situation and it looks really bad. But when we reflect on the Word, we know that God is using it and working it out for our good.

I have often asked, "Lord what are we going to do with this?" because I know the situation is going to be for my good one way or another. I know God is going to use it. So wherever I find myself in any given point in life, I know that God is at work. Either He is preparing me for something to come, or He is equipping me for this present time.

"Great is our Lord, and of great power: his understanding is infinite" (Psalm 147:5 KJV). We can rejoice that God is sovereign. We can be confident that God knows. He has a plan for our lives, and He is going to do an awesome work in our midst. As we believe God's Word and obey His instructions, He will enable us to maximize our marriages. As we play our part in God's plan, He causes us to move from faith to faith, from strength to strength, and from glory to glory.

Let us pray.

> *Dear Lord, I thank You that Your Word has fallen on good ground and that something in these pages will be helpful in our lives. Lord, I pray that You would continue to change, equip, and empower us. Enable us to maximize our marriage relationships and to endure to the end, doing the will of God in every situation.*
>
> *In Jesus' name I pray. Amen.*

CHAPTER FIVE

Seeking
Counseling—Finding
Solutions

We often consider our churches to be places of refuge for those who are wounded, but it seems too often that instead of helping, we shoot our wounded. The Bible is clear that we are to comfort others with the comfort that we ourselves have received. "Blessed be God, even the Father of our Lord Jesus Christ, the Father of mercies, and the God of all comfort; who comforteth us in all our tribulation, that we may be able to comfort them which are in any trouble, by the comfort wherewith we ourselves are comforted of God" (2 Corinthians 1:3–4 KJV). Therefore, we must become prepared to offer care and encouragement to those in unequally yoked relationships, who are wounded and in need of hope, help, and healing.

When you are in an unequally yoked relationship, you are definitely searching for those who know how to minister to you. You need support, prayer, and fellowship. Anything that the church can offer to promote a sense of community and belonging or that individual believers can do to meet one of these needs is a great opportunity for ministry.

Fourteen years ago, the church was indeed a place of solace for me. I was glad to be around people who were excited about the things of God because that was not the reality in my household. So I was always running to the church because that is where I thought people would love me most. However, I soon found that the church was not a safe haven for me. I felt alienated and excluded. It seemed that the church was not sensitive to people like me, those in unequally yoked marriages.

There are many groups in the church. But where is the place for those who are unequally yoked? Since I went to the church alone, initially people thought that I was single. So the singles' group invited me to all of their events. However, one of the goals of this group was to build relationships for dating and future marriage. When I went to a singles' event, I gave the impression that I was available when, in fact, I was not. So although I was alone, I felt out of place at singles' events.

When the couples had an activity planned, I initially got excited. But then I realized my spouse was not coming. And showing up alone among all the other happy couples would be embarrassing, and I felt even more isolated. So what was I supposed to do? Where was I supposed to I go? More often than not, I simply went back home to the hostile environment. You would think that I would have been better off feeling isolated with the couples. At least at the couples' functions I was evenly yoked!

WHAT MATTERS MOST

In 1995, a study was done examining the impact of religious harmony (equal yokes) on the stability of and satisfaction in marital relationships. The study indicated that women had a higher degree of religious commitment (i.e., they attended church more often, read the Bible more intensely, prayed more frequently, and had an overall higher spiritual base) than men. Although women had a higher degree of spirituality, it was their spouses' spiritual commitment (or lack thereof) that affected the stability of the marriage the most. Like so many women in unequally yoked marriages, I was more interested in cultivating my relationship with the Lord, and my husband spent his time watching me and finding fault. It took me a while (a long while), but I learned that the most important thing for me to do was to please God. All that "perfect wife" stuff that I was doing was not getting me anywhere—with José or with God. Mostly because I was forcing myself to be something that I had not grown into and both God and José knew it! So I was more of a phony than anything. What I learned was that God was the person that I needed to please. Pleasing God would lead to the peace that I really longed for. And my husband would have to make his own peace with God whenever. In short, his growth was between him and God, not me!

In my work, I have found that although many of us are growing in the Lord (e.g., by reading the word and going to church) we would rather that our spouses grow and be nurtured in the things of God. This is what makes women happy in marriage. I know that I was ecstatic when José began to show interest in the things of God. Then I realized that it was very important for me shift my focus from just pleasing him, to pleasing Him—pleasing God the Father. As I began to please God and serve Him, José automatically benefited and the marriage eventually improved.

THE NEED FOR COUNSELING

You should seriously consider marriage counseling to guide you through the turmoil of your relationship. When you go in for counseling, most counselors do an initial assessment to gather basic data and information. This procedure, usually called a "bio-psycho-social" assessment, covers three areas: biological, psychological, and social. As a practicing Christian counselor, when clients first come in, I do a "bio-psycho-social-spiritual," which also includes a very important spiritual assessment. I want to know: What about your spirituality? What is your source of faith, strength, or power when you are in darkness or despair? When you need hope and encouragement, where do you turn? What do you do? Are you a person of prayer? Do you have a scriptural text? Do you have a support system? The answers to these questions often provide an indication of what this person may be dealing with in their marriage and if they are applying biblical principles to help them cope.

I have sat on both sides of the table; I've been the person seeking counseling as well as the one providing hope and encouragement to others who are seeking counsel. People don't walk into a counseling office and say, "I am unequally yoked. I need help." I didn't. Instead, they say, "I'm depressed. I don't know why. I just don't feel good. Things aren't going well. I'm not sleeping. I'm not eating. I cry a lot." However, when they begin to talk about the spiritual imbalance in their marriage, I understand more clearly why they are experiencing certain problems. There are some common, basic concerns that come up in counseling people who are in unequally yoked marriages. Yet you can grow spiritually through all of them.

From my experience as the helper and the one needing help, I've learned some practical strategies to help you and your spouse walk out your Christian faith in wisdom through the power of God. Some of the most common issues include anger, depression, envy, loneliness, low self-esteem, and submission. Let me share with you some of the insights I've learned about these topics.

Anger — is either fear or frustration

There are many situations that can produce anger in the hearts of women (and men). Sometimes women in unequally yoked relationships are angry with themselves. They experience anger and self-hatred because they cannot believe the things they have allowed

102

themselves to put up with.

Millie was once very active in her church and community. Hank was jealous of everyone she spent any time with doing anything. Slowly over the years people stopped calling her and coming by her house. She was no longer invited to participate on various committees and projects. When she finally asked someone what happened, she was informed that Hank interrogated everyone who called (including her own family). People were frightened for her because of Hank's temper, so they just stayed away. It was two years later when Millie came in for counseling. "You know, I cannot believe that I have allowed myself to be held captive in this marriage all this time." She went on to tell me how she really loved Hank and wanted the marriage to work. "I should have sought help before now, because all I can think of is getting out." I had certainly felt like Millie. But I thank God that He kept me through it all. Had I not truly loved José, I would have gotten out as well. Moreover, if we were not friends from the start, I would have abandoned the relationship after year two.

Nevertheless, I was angry with myself and sometimes I was angry with people at my church. It seemed to me that they would have noticed that I was married, but no one said anything to me. Nobody invited me over. Perhaps they did not think that I fit in with the couples because my husband didn't attend church. It seemed to me that they would have realized that I did not fit in with the singles either. Someone could have invited me over for a meal, or just to fellowship.

I kept thinking, "You guys talk such good talk. But where is your real witness?" They all seemed so unresponsive. I was hurting Sunday after Sunday and desperately wanting someone to talk with me. But I found that on the traditional Sunday morning everybody was passing everybody else very quickly saying, "Hi, how is it going? How are you doing? I am blessed. Are you blessed?" Like everyone else, I learned to smile and say, "Oh, I am blessed of the Lord." Unfortunately, for far too long, I really did not feel blessed. And my being a Christian did not positively affect my situation. But whom was I going to tell? And who was going to stand still long enough to listen? So I had to deal with my anger alone. The superficial fellowship and relationships with the believers at my church did not help matters. I was left to suffer alone—married, yet detached—by myself, but not single. And I was angry because I was expecting the church members to notice my distress and come to my rescue. This did not happen.

I was also angry with the church leadership, and the Bible. I felt like a woman who had been battered into submission and that leadership was collaborating with a religious system that more or less demanded that I stay there and take it! In this situation, what recourse did I have? Of course, I knew all the Scriptures to support my situation, but it was difficult living with what seemed to me like an abuse of power and an abuse of God's Word. Bottom line, I was angry with the leaders of the church, the Bible, and with God.

I was angry at the injustice and unfairness of it all. "How did I get stuck in this situation?" In my mind, I had been a good person all of my life. I had done the right thing. I followed God. "It's not fair. Why me? I don't deserve this."

Depression

Like many women in unbalanced marriages, I experienced situational depression. Basically, I was depressed because I was married to a man who did not know God. Similarly, Anita had been depressed for so long that it had become a way of life. She couldn't even remember when she first began to feel so sad. Depressed women may go from one extreme to the other. Some women sleep the days away so that they don't have to feel the pain of loneliness; others run on adrenaline nonstop, involving themselves in one activity after another. Some women continuously eat to ease their emotions. Whenever they experience discomfort they go to the refrigerator to stuff the feeling.

Marjorie had gained thirty pounds in two months before she acknowledged that she was depressed. She had stopped crying herself to sleep some time earlier; instead whenever she felt sad she would have a big bowl of ice cream to help her feel better. Sometimes she would even enjoy a slice of cake or two with her ice cream. The back seat of her car was cluttered with candy wrappers and empty fast-food bags. Whenever she felt any emotion she would suppress it with food. When Marjorie came in for counseling she wanted help with her diet. In reality, what she needed was to allow God to help her process her pain and to feed on His Word for comfort.

LaDonna, on the other hand, was wasting away. She had lost twenty-five pounds in three weeks. Her friends were commending her for the discipline she used to lose weight. She really looked good when she lost the first ten pounds. People started to worry when she continued to drastically lose more and more. This amazed everyone, especially her husband, since she cooked "Sunday dinner" kinds of meals daily: big pots of greens, cornbread, macaroni and cheese, yams, and roast beef. Her family ate well, but LaDonna was so depressed she didn't have an appetite. Without much thought, she carried out her responsibilities as a wife, mother, and homemaker. When some women are depressed, they are not motivated to do chores or anything else, including those things they would normally enjoy doing. When someone exhibits any of these signs or symptoms for a period of two weeks or more, they should seek counseling. Even those who have functioned for years while suffering from depression should also seek help.

Envy

Envy is a common issue for women who are in unequally yoked marriages. Envy usually results from a perception problem—from seeing all of the other "happy" couples. Think about it. On Sunday morning at church, there is Mr. and Mrs. Smith. They are sitting there all cuddled up and hugged up. And then Mr. and Mrs. Jones, they are holding hands. Mr. and Mrs. Abernathy, they are smiling and gazing into each other's eyes the whole time. And then there you are—sitting all alone on the pew.

I found out later that the Smiths were having problems and the Joneses were basically keeping up with the Abernathys. They were keeping up the pretense. I learned that while a couple looks happy to others, especially women like me, they are oftentimes struggling to keep a lid on things. Some of these couples fight and argue on their way to church or on the way back home.

Now, I am not saying that Christians don't have happy marriages—they really do. Those with happy marriages know how to resolve their issues. They have made a commitment to solve their problems God's way. This shared commitment is usually what an unequally yoked marital relationship may be lacking.

My point in making these observations was that I saw what I wanted to see. Because my situation was so bleak, my depression wreaked havoc with me, as I over-romanticized what was going on in other relationships. Struggling with envy, I often looked around and thought, "You know, he seems like such a good husband. I always see him with the kids. I always see him pulling up in the car to pick her up at the door after church on Sunday." In comparison, I thought, "She has all of this, and I have nothing. Their lives look so wonderful, and look at poor me. If only my husband were saved, we would have that happy marriage that everybody else has."

lie

Loneliness

There is intense isolation in an unequally yoked marriage. Much of this isolation is self-inflicted. I didn't have many friends, by choice, because I felt like I didn't fit in.

Once when I was crying out to God saying, "Poor me. Poor me. I'm so lonely," God said, "Well, get a friend." And I said, "Well, give me one." He said, "You have a whole church full of people; pick one." I finally started thinking, "OK, there are some things I need to do."

What I did was to take responsibility and take action. Too many of you are like I was: sitting at home, crying the blues, waiting on God to zap your husband and zap the church and change your whole situation—when instead all that is needed is to become actively involved in the process of what God is already doing—working things out for good.

In my case, I really didn't want anybody to know how bad my situation was. It became easier to keep people at a distance. I smiled and laughed and talked with everybody, but kept moving. They were passing me, and I was passing them because I did not want anybody to stop me and ask, "Sabrina, where is your husband?"

I didn't want to explain that at that time, he was my "heathen husband"—by his own profession. For my husband, it was almost a joke: "Oh, I have this great Christian wife, and I am her heathen husband." I would plead, "Honey, please stop saying that." People would call and he would answer the phone: "This is heathen head-quarters." Looking back on it now I can laugh, but at the time I thought, "You may find this funny, but I am not amused."

Even though allowing them to enter into my world (to see inside my home life) was challenging, when God prompted me to develop relationships in the church, I did. Over the years, I met together with women of similar circumstances. We were that much-needed support that each had sought at various points in our marriages. I facilitated or was part of several different groups—Daughters of Abigail, Joyful Meeting, Creative Counterparts, Sisters of Sarah, and BLESSED—that really ministered to my needs. We spent time sharing how God was blessing us through our struggles; we encouraged and admonished one another to live in accordance with the Word of God, and we prayed for our husbands, our households, and each other. As we shifted our focus, we began to see the power and results of a praying wife.

Low Self-Esteem

Some women deal with low self-esteem because of a misunderstanding of Scripture. In the Amplified Bible, 1 Peter 3:1 says, "In like manner, you married women, be submissive to your own husbands [subordinate yourselves as being secondary to and dependent on them, and adapt yourselves to them], so that even if any do not obey the Word [of God], they may be won over not by discussion but by the [godly] lives of their wives."

Again, this passage says the husband "may be won." Unfortunately, some women take that to mean that he will definitely be won. So when their husbands remain unsaved they think, "I must be a failure. It must be something that I'm doing wrong. What more can I do? What else do I need to do so that he will come to know the Lord?" It was years before José accepted Christ. I remember an occasion when I had been a Christian for six years and someone asked about his salvation. The look I received when I told them he was not saved seemed to imply that it was my fault. Certainly if I were a better or more submissive wife, he would "be won" by now.

Many women have been made to feel inadequate and unworthy. Often women who are in unequally yoked marriages receive a lot of ridicule and criticism from their spouse. "Yeah right, you go to church—so what? You read your Bible—so what? Your life does not look any different to me." These women need to look to God for significance and value. They must come to the place where they can say, "God is my witness. I know I am changing. It may only be a little bit at a time, but I know I am growing. And it is God who will open my husband's eyes so he can see that. It won't necessarily be something specific that I do. I can't paint a big sign that says: Look, I Am A Christian Now. Eventually, he is going to see the difference in my lifestyle because I am going to be a living epistle" (2 Corinthians 3:3).

We can stop our epitaphs of suffering and find out what we can do to empower our lives—to glorify God with triumphant marriages. We can stop our "woe is me" stories today and look more closely at what God has to say about His chosen vessels, who are precious and honored in His sight.

Submission

In counseling, you find women who have been battered into submission. It is never a biblical situation of honor, reverence, and respect when a woman must submit to her husband because she has no choice. It is not God's plan for any woman to be forced to do things that she would not normally do in her right mind. In fact, this type of situation could be considered "spiritual abuse." It is deplorable that there can be spiritual abuse in a marriage relationship, but it does exist—especially in unequally yoked marriages.

There is a lot of confusion surrounding the teaching on submission. You can read books, attend workshops, and go to classes on submission and still not be willing to submit. Submission is a heart attitude. It is not a list of "things to do" or a situation where you begrudgingly just "do what you are told." Biblical submission involves a spirit of reverence and admiration. It requires a "wanting to," not because of who you are or who your spouse is, but because of who God is. Scripture states, "Wives, submit yourselves unto your own husbands, as unto the Lord" (Ephesians 5:22 KJV). We are reminded the same thing again in Colossians 3:18, "Wives, submit yourselves unto your own husbands, as it is fit in the Lord" (KJV).

Women often ask, "Well, what if he tells me to do something that is ungodly?" Then don't be foolish. God has given you a good mind. Do not do anything that is illegal, immoral, or illicit; don't do anything that violates Scripture. But when the things he asks you to do (or not to do) don't violate Scripture, do them as unto the Lord.

Much of the anxiety that I experienced was the result of needless worry because I did not want to submit to his leadership. I worried about what José would say when he found out, for example, that I made this financial commitment to the church, or heard about something that I said to the pastor. One of the things that I had to learn was to be open and honest. Then I would not have to worry about what would happen when he found out. It took awhile, but I finally stopped keeping secrets. I started telling him what I was planning. And when he said "no," I accepted "no" as the answer. Mind you, this took some time.

I had wanted to go to Africa for at least three or four years. Every year when it was time to start raising money for the missions trip, I would go to my husband and say, "What do you think? They have this great opportunity for missions work in Africa coming up. I can start raising support!" And he would ask, "Why do you want to go to Africa? You have all these people over here you need to save." I would try to explain the biblical concept of missions and what we were going there to do. He was not convinced.

My first thought was, "I shouldn't have told him. I should have just made the plans and then said, 'I have to go now. I've put up the deposit money.'" But that would have been deceptive and dishonest. Instead, I accepted the fact that my husband had said "no," so I could not go. When I asked the following year, he said "no" again. "The political climate is not such that you should be over there. They may keep you over there, and you may not get back home." After three years of receiving "no" as an answer, you would think I would have stopped asking. But I knew in my heart, even then, that God had called me to make a local and global impact. I wanted to go, and I knew that the Lord wanted me there. It was simply a matter of timing. When I asked the fourth time, my husband said, "Yeah, you should go. Call this person, and this person, and this person. I know they will give you money to go." I shouted, "Amen, Lord!" because it was God's doing in His timing.

God can work through your unsaved spouse (and even faster, as you submit). God has a season for everything. But we must obey God during the process. Honesty and obedience, as you submit with joy in reverence to your spouse, will eliminate some of the unnecessary worry and anxiety.

SEEKING COUNSELING

There are many different therapeutic approaches for counseling those who are unequally yoked. Just having someone to talk to about your experiences and your emotions can be very helpful. This gives you a much-needed chance to clear your head, think about your thinking, and examine the motives behind your behavior. "As a man (or woman) thinks in his heart, so is he" (Proverbs 23:7a paraphrased). What you think will eventually be acted out in your behavior. I try to help women understand what others (including myself) have learned the hard way.

If you are constantly thinking good thoughts about your spouse, when given the opportunity, you are going to say good things. But if you are always thinking about what you don't like, what you wish would change, how unhappy you are, or how this isn't right; then, when given the opportunity, those are the things you are going to say. "For out of the abundance of the heart, the mouth speaks" (Luke 6:45 paraphrased).

Bill and Sherri's marriage had been shaky for years. Bill drank beer during the week and the hard stuff on the weekends. When he did, he was verbally and emotionally abusive. Sherri felt trapped by her vows "until death do us part." She didn't see a reason to seek counseling. In her mind, there was nothing that anyone could do. Instead Sherri would often plot ways to kill Bill, although she never intended to ever execute any of these methods. In the mid-

111

dle of a heated argument about Bill's drinking, Sherri blurted out her secret wish—"I'd be better off if you just drank yourself to death."

People say negative things and think, "I really didn't mean that. I don't know where it came from." It came from your heart. It has been in your spirit all this time and this was an opportunity for it to come out. Whenever you find yourself consistently thinking unbiblical or irrational thoughts, it's time to seek help.

Some of the irrational thoughts of people in unequally yoked marriages that cause problems include, but are not limited to, the following:

- "I must save my spouse. If my spouse is not saved, then I must be a failure." Women who believe these statements feel that it is absolutely necessary that they convince their husband to believe in and live for God. They think, "I have done everything I can think of. I have done everything he has asked me to do. I have done everything all of my friends have suggested, as well as what the magazines and the talk show hosts have indicated. I have done everything—the good stuff, the bad stuff, and the stuff in between—nothing seems to work. It must be me—I am a failure."

  We cannot save anyone else. We are not that powerful. God drew us, wooed us, loved us, and brought us into His kingdom. The only things we can do are to pray and live our lives before our spouse in such a way that God is glorified.

- "I must be the perfect spouse." Some women feel that the perfect spouse cleans the house twice a day, cooks gourmet meals, has sex on demand, and caters to her husband's every whim. Others try to become whatever their husband thinks perfection might be. They jump through hoops and bend over backwards, and they end up being miserable and frustrated because they don't see the response or get the results they are expecting.

112

Perfection is hard to define and impossible to attain. Only God is perfect. Instead of trying to be the perfect spouse, the goal should be to live a life that pleases God and let your spouse be blessed in the process. Our goal is to become more like Christ.

■ "I cannot grow and do things without my spouse." There are far too many women who have basically just withered away; they have lost their sense of individuality. It is almost as if they are joined at the hip to their spouses. When he does not want to do anything, they feel condemned to stay at home for the rest of their lives. They think, "I have no choice. I can't do anything. I can't grow."

Every individual is personally responsible for his or her own growth and maturity in God. Each of us needs to be doing the things of God regardless of what our spouse is doing. We can help people in unequally yoked relationships by helping them understand that they need to continue growing spiritually as much as they can. It is their relationship with God that will sustain them through difficult situations.

Harboring irrational beliefs dramatically reduces the level of satisfaction and contentment in marriage. Therefore, women must focus on changing their thoughts and the resulting behavior.

LIVING IN REALITY

It is important that men and women in unequally yoked marriages face reality, live realistically, and assume responsibility for how they live their lives. Start by exploring and assessing your wants, needs, and desires. If you don't like where your life is heading, stop and go in a different direction. Evaluate your behavior, examine the direction of your life, and then make plans to change. You don't have to keep following the same old path over and over again. One definition of "crazy" is doing the same thing over and over again and expecting different results. When you reach this point, you really do need help—you need to learn to do something different. If you are jumping through hoops and bending over backwards and your husband still is not satisfied, and the marriage is not getting any better, and you are becoming depressed because you have done everything you can think of—Stop! Do those things that God has called you to do and stop trying to do everything under the sun.

On Judgment Day, every man and woman will give an account of every thought, every word, and every deed (Matthew 12:36; Romans 14:12; 2 Corinthians 5:10). We each are responsible for our own actions; stop blaming your spouse for your behavior. Not everything is your spouse's fault. Life might be better if he or she would only change. But even if your mate doesn't change, your perspective can and probably needs to.

As a counselor, I make the most of every opportunity with my clients. When what they are saying sounds inappropriate to me, I tell them. Sometimes there is no nice way to say, "You are totally out of line. Your behavior is unbiblical. That is not based on Scripture." And I may not have three or four sessions, three or four months, or three or four years to get to that point.

I do not believe counseling should take a person's lifetime. My approach tends to be brief-focused/solution-oriented. My goal is to enable women to use the tools God has provided for them and to deal with whatever it is that God has sent them to counseling to address. I confront my clients because I care and also because there is a sense of urgency. The Day of the Lord is drawing near.

WHEN YOUR SPOUSE RECEIVES COUNSEL

While both men and women in unequally yoked relationships struggle with similar issues, it is the women who most often seek counseling. By the grace of God, when I counsel a woman who is unequally yoked, I often get her spouse to come in for counseling as well. As a rule, men do not like to come in for counseling. First of all, they don't want anybody telling them what to do or how to run their household. Nor do they want to be perceived as the one with the problem or the one who is causing the problem in the marriage relationship. In addition, it is very rare that you get an African-American male to agree to counseling. But God has given me favor, and one way or another my clients' husbands usually come in for an initial session and more. In fact, they are usually glad to come in when they find out why.

My technique is simple. I send an invitation home with the client requesting that her husband attend a counseling session to help me help her. I do not say, "You have a problem. You need to get saved. You need to get fixed. We want to evangelize you so that she can live a better life." Instead, I simply invite him to help me help his wife. Men love that. I can imagine them thinking, "I would be more than happy to come and tell you all the stuff that she is not doing." I warn my client to expect this type of attitude up front. I clearly explain to her my intentions and ask her to not be offended. I let her know that "the goal of the session is not to bash you, beat you up, or point out all your faults." But her husband may say some clear and valid things that she may have missed. He may explain why he refuses to have anything to do with the church, why he does not like church people, or why he thinks she is a hypocrite. She has an opportunity in our next counseling session to process whatever it is he had to say.

Think of it from his point of view. Here is somebody who is actually offering to listen to him. When her husband comes in, he has the entire counseling session to say whatever he wants to say. I take notes and I ask his wife to sit and listen. As we close the session, I ask, "Would you be willing to come back and help me out again in the future?" Men like to be helpful. He usually says, "Yes, call me whenever you need me." Because of his positive experience, he is willing to come back again. Very often, the client's husband not only wants to talk about his wife, but he wants to come back and talk about himself. I frequently hear, "You know, I have a few things I may want to talk about. Can I make an appointment?" My answer is always, "Absolutely."

PRACTICAL STRATEGIES FOR FINDING SOLUTIONS

In addition to *Christian counseling,* there are many other *practical strategies* that can be used to help people in unequally yoked relationships find solutions to the problems they may face.

Practical Strategy #1—Promoting the Development of Ministry Groups in the Church

Our churches are filled with people who are in unequally yoked relationships. However, they often cannot find a place for fellowship and so their needs go unrecognized. This lack of recognition makes it difficult, if not impossible, for them to receive the help and encouragement they desperately need from the very people who should understand their situation the most.

By developing Christian fellowship groups for those who are unequally yoked, the church can become more inclusive and better able to effectively minister to this special population. Such church ministry and support groups should have specific goals, not limited to but including:

- *Growing spiritually*

- *Understanding the marriage relationship*

- *Building self-esteem by helping individuals recognize their value and significance*

- *Solving problems and changing self-defeating thoughts and behavior*

- *Dropping pretenses, making choices, acknowledging and expressing your feelings*

- *Gaining control and restoring personal happiness and fulfillment*

The church must also address the need for the congregation to become more sensitive and better equipped to offer care and encouragement to members of this special population.

Practical Strategy #2—Developing Personal Coping Strategies

Anyone who has been in an unequally yoked marriage (even early in the relationship) has learned to cope. As a counselor, you can help them identify their strengths by asking questions. "How is it that you have been able to handle this situation so far? What are you doing that is working? What are you doing that is not working and needs to change?"

Practical Strategy #3—Accepting Responsibility

Helping women accept responsibility for how they live and helping them realize that they do indeed have a choice is of primary importance. Women always have a choice. And they need to know that. They can choose to be in bondage or choose to walk in the freedom for which Christ died. It is their choice. They should understand that if Christ has set them free, no one should have them in bondage again. Scripture says we are not to become entangled again with the yoke of bondage. "Stand fast therefore in the liberty wherewith Christ hath made us free, and be not entangled again with the yoke of bondage" (Galatians 5:1 KJV). This verse, literally interpreted, means bondage to legalism. Women should not be forced to follow the Law but learn to embrace the spirit of the Law. If they become entangled, that is their choice. Jesus came that the captives might be free (Isaiah 61:1; Luke 4:18), and this freedom is available to all who belong to Jesus Christ. Christian women in unequally yoked relationships must learn to choose freedom and walk in it.

Practical Strategy #4—Establishing Boundaries

Some women unrealistically try to carry out their own responsibilities, their spouses' responsibilities, and the responsibilities of ministry at the church. For example, a husband comes home from work and is told, "I have set up an appointment for you to meet with my pastor and talk with him." Her husband didn't want an appointment and the pastor didn't really have the time. But she is negotiating and setting up things. Instead, these women should be encouraged to refocus on their responsibility and concentrate on what they need to do.

Practical Strategy #5—Ministering at Home

Our actions are often driven by our basic needs. We all want to be accepted; we want to be affiliated with something, and we want to be admired. We spend our lives trying to figure out how to obtain or achieve the things that we want most. So if you are looking for attention, affection, and affiliation, you are going to go where you will receive it. For a lot of women, that is the church.

During my third and fourth years of marriage, I had such a need for affirmation, affiliation, and attention that I wanted to do whatever I could in the church to meet that need. I think the best advice my pastor gave me was when he sent me home. He said, "Home is where your ministry needs to be. The church will run without you; your marriage won't." That is hard to accept, but it is the reality in all marriages.

Women are needed at home. Scripture tells us that a prophet is not always welcome in his own hometown. "But Jesus said unto them, A prophet is not without honour, but in his own country, and among his own kin, and in his own house" (Mark 6:4 KJV). However, ministry must still take place there. You are best acquainted with the people in your home, so you need to minister there. Ministering to your spouse is indeed very honorable in the sight of the Lord. "Marriage is honorable in all, and the bed undefiled" (Hebrews 13:4a KJV). As a woman ministers at home, she becomes a vessel through which God's blessings are channeled.

Practical Strategy #6—Studying the Word

The Word of God is there to help you. The Bible says that "all Scripture is God-breathed" (2 Timothy 3:16a NIV). That means the entire Word of God is useful, beneficial, and profitable so that men and women of God can be thoroughly equipped and adequately furnished for every good work (2 Timothy 3:16–17 paraphrased). As you open the Word of God, whatever page you turn to, wherever the Bible falls open, whatever you read, you can use. God's Word will be useful to teach you something, to correct you in a particular area, to rebuke, reprove, or train you in righteousness.

When studying the Word, it is often best to keep it simple. Ask yourself some basic questions like, "What did it say? What does it mean? And what am I supposed to do in light of that?" When we take hold of these things—what the Word of God says, what it means, and how to live according to it—our lives will change.

Reading the Bible does not have to be intimidating. If you are unfamiliar with it, utilize the table of contents and study aids. These resources will be helpful in finding and understanding books in the Bible such as Haggai, Habakkuk, or Zephaniah. If you are not sure where to begin, start reading the Psalms or Proverbs; these books are filled with praise, prayer, and wisdom. There are 31 chapters in Proverbs, so you could read one chapter of Proverbs each day. If you forget for a day or two, do not beat yourself up about it. Just continue with the chapter in Proverbs that matches the day of the month. If today is the 17th, read Proverbs 17. If you forget for a couple of days, and it is now the 20th, read Proverbs chapter 20. This simple method makes it easy for a beginner to get into the habit of reading the Word.

I strongly urge every believer to study the Word daily—at least get into the habit of picking up the Bible every day and reading something. When giving reading assignments to clients, I also find that Bible stories are very helpful. People can identify with and relate to the characters and situations in the stories. For some people, this method of Bible study may be more effective than memorizing several Bible verses out of context. Remember, the objective is not following a method of study but gaining an understanding of Scripture. Therefore, the reader should always ask, "Now that I have read this, how do I apply it? What am I supposed to do?"

Practical Strategy #7—Persevering in Prayer

There is power in prayer. It has been said that prayer not only changes the situation; it changes you. When you pray for a person, your perception of them changes. Your heart is not as hard toward a person when you pray for them. It is hard to be angry, bitter, and mad at somebody and say, "Lord, bless him or her."

In working with women, you need to constantly ask them, "What is it that God is saying to you?" If they do not know, they need to be in prayer even more so. God is always speaking. We need to help women to see what God is doing and hear what God is saying.

Women also need to be reminded that their battle is not against flesh and blood. Their husband is not the enemy. "For we wrestle not against flesh and blood, but against principalities, against powers, against the rulers of the darkness of this world, against spiritual wickedness in high places" (Ephesians 6:12 KJV). So when problems occur, they need to intensify the level of prayer at that point. Everything we do should be undergirded by prayer. I cannot emphasize enough the importance of communing with God—talking to Him and listening to His response.

Practical Strategy #8—Trusting the Sovereignty of God

Our God reigns. We need to stop telling God about our problems and start telling our problems about God. Our God, who is awesome and powerful, active and available, is much bigger than our problems. God already knows all about our situation. We need to focus on God and begin to speak life into our situation based on His Word. Nothing happens by accident to the children of God.

Practical Strategy #9—Doing What Is Right

In the New Testament alone, there are over forty-seven different references to how we need to respond one to another. It talks about showing one another hospitality, greeting one another with a holy kiss, greeting one another with a hug, esteeming one another more highly than ourselves, not grumbling against one another, honoring one another; it just goes on and on and on. I often hear people say, "Well, if my spouse was saved, I would do this, this, and this." I reply, "Treat them like God treats you. Bless them. Be good to them because of your relationship with God and your desire to apply the Word in your marriage."

Practical Strategy #10—Walking in the Spirit

Scripture tells us "if we walk in the Spirit, we will not fulfill the lusts of the flesh" (Galatians 5:16 paraphrased). You cannot walk both ways. Anytime you are doing something that is outside of the will of God, you know that you are not walking in the Spirit. To encourage women to stay balanced, start with a routine checkup. Ask, "How were you walking last week? Were you walking your talk? Were you doing a wisdom walk? Were you applying the Word of God in your life?"

Practical Strategy #11—Remembering the Full Circle of Marriage

Many women in unequally yoked marriage relationships mistakenly believe that their marriage can never be successful or satisfying. They think that because they disagree on the necessity or level of religious commitment, they will be unable to agree on anything else. However, that is a defeatist attitude. Spirituality is an important part of marriage, but there are many other things that go into making up a full, vital marriage relationship. Remembering the full circle of marriage is a real challenge; it does not happen by accident.

When I first got saved, Christ, the Bible, the church, and spiritual aspects of life were the only things I thought about. I just became this big spiritual person. I forgot about the rest of my marriage. I kept thinking, "My husband and I really don't have anything in common. I love the Lord, and he loves the world." When he talked about going out and doing something recreational, I didn't want to go with him. I couldn't imagine him going anyplace that I would want to go. All of the people that we used to call friends were unsaved, so I didn't want to be around them anymore. Why would a spouse want to change if the only examples of spirituality were from a wife who was no longer fun to be with?

In addition to the spiritual dimension of marriage, there are also parental, financial, relational, psychological, volitional (which is your will), emotional, physical, recreational, and vocational aspects of the marriage relationship, as well. Unfortunately, I was stuck on religion and didn't have time for anything else. I just kept thinking, "If my husband isn't saved, then the marriage cannot work. If my husband isn't saved, how can we go out and have fun? What kind of relationship could we have? I don't know if I should tithe or not tithe. What should I do with my money? Should I ask him for money from his check?" For me, the marriage relationship was almost in a cloud. If it didn't say religion in front of it or if I couldn't find a verse for it, then it wasn't relevant.

When I started to identify basic marriage problems as yoke problems, I also discovered that my problems had more to do with my negative attitude and my approach toward my husband than with his relationship (or lack of relationship) with Christ. The Lord began to deal with me and show me how self-righteous I had become. Then I was able to go back and try to approach my husband again, to ask for forgiveness in certain areas, to try to rebuild our relationship, and to rediscover the other areas of our marriage that did work.

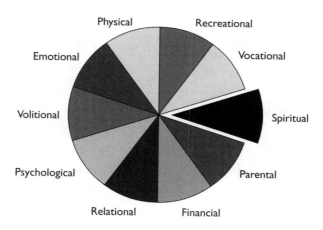

The Full Circle of Marriage
Areas of Focus

Figure 5-1

If you look at the top of the diagram, you will see that there are equal parts in this circle of life. Consequently, there is a lot more to marriage than just the religious aspect. You don't want to get stuck in one place thinking, "Because my husband isn't saved, nothing else matters." You can develop intimacy and togetherness in other areas. There are other things that you can do. Remember the full circle of marriage, and see where you can expand your relationship. Ask yourself, "What happened to these other areas of my marriage? Do I need to go back and work on some things?"

Practical Strategy #12—Walking in Agreement

We tend to go out and make decisions on our own. For example, have you ever discussed with your husband whether or not you should work? Or did you just decide, "I want to work. I want to have some money of my own. There are some things I want to do. So my money is my money and your money is yours. We can pay the bills out of yours, but I will spend mine"? Sometimes we have to catch ourselves and hear the psychology behind what we are saying.

Marriage is a relationship; it is not about separatism. God has called a wife to be a helpmate to her husband. "And the Lord God said, It is not good that the man should be alone; I will make him an help meet for him" (Genesis 2:18 KJV). But when you are thinking only of yourself, spiritual things, or issues of mine and yours, it's hard to be helpful. There are times when you must choose between your desires and your principles—when going after what you want would damage what you believe in and stand for.

My husband was so glad when I finally came to the realization that I was supposed to help. He was relieved to know that I cared enough to want to help out. I wish that I could say that I told him, "Honey, I realize how hard you are working to make ends meet. I know that I am an expensive habit. Beyond the bills, just maintaining me alone is more than a notion. Thank you so much—not just for working one job but for working those extra overtime hours." No, instead I thought, "That is what you are supposed to do. You are the man of the house. To provide and take care of your wife and household is your job." Learning that I also had a part to play came much later.

We really have to watch our attitudes and how we respond to

the man or woman that God has placed in our lives. We must learn to work together. In fact, we must be willing to work at it because walking in agreement may not happen overnight. Each couple will need to identify what will work for them.

Practical Strategy #13—Reaffirming Your Commitment

It is indeed a high calling to be in an unequally yoked marriage relationship. Not everyone can handle it. Some women say, "Well, I do not know if God placed this man in my life. This might have been an accident. When we got married, I didn't know any better; we weren't saved. If I had to do this all over again, I don't know."

To counter this attitude, I often encourage clients to spend more time looking at the things they saw in their husband when they first met him. Take time to remember what attracted you to him in the first place. There was a reason why you got married. Some people were married because there was a child involved. Maybe you wanted your child to have a father in the home. Even if that was your only reason, many of the characteristics it takes to be a good father are similar to those needed to become a good husband. But now that you have him, regardless of why you have him, you can learn to love and honor him.

When my husband asks me, "Would you marry me again?" the answer is an emphatic "Yes!" I really would. I love the man. I have learned to look beyond his faults the way God looks beyond mine. I have learned to look past all the little things—like picking up clothes (even though he picks up after me). It is those little things that become annoying when they occur on a regular basis and make you think, "Will I ever get through this?" Instead, I ask God to help me see all that my husband will become. I plan to hang in here until the end, and he knows that. I believe in marriage until death do us part. The key is not to kill each other in the process.

Practical Strategy #14—Being Yoked with Jesus

Finally, we must encourage both men and women in unequally yoked relationships to remember the impact that Christ makes in their life and marriage. It is their relationship with Jesus Christ that must be first, and it makes all the difference. Being yoked together with Jesus means that God's power is active and available to bring them through the difficult times. "Who shall separate us from the love of Christ? shall tribulation, or distress, or persecution, or famine, or nakedness, or peril, or sword? Nay, in all these things we are more than conquerors through him that loved us" (Romans 8:35, 37 KJV).

Let's pray.

> *Dear Lord, I thank You for my brothers and sisters who may need to seek counsel or who will have an opportunity to minister to those who are unequally yoked. I pray that the things they have read will make a difference in their lives and in the lives of those they come into contact with. May they accept the challenge and become better equipped to minister to others. In Jesus' name we pray. Amen.*

Prayer Request + Praise
Cherri's Funk - get out
Roger's interview
Tina's Son
For Courtney

CHAPTER SIX

Mr. & Ms.— Communication in Marriage

I remember vividly the day that Mr. and Mrs. Johnson quietly entered the counseling session. They avoided the couch and took chairs on opposite sides of the room. After briefly reviewing their admission forms, I asked them to tell me the key issue for which they were seeking counsel. Mrs. Johnson stared at her husband and intently began her discourse. "He always . . . he should . . . he never . . . he knows . . . we believe . . . we think . . . we feel . . . we want . . . we have . . . we need." She went on and on and on for approximately fifteen to twenty minutes before she took a deep breath and asked me, "Well, what do you think?" She had shared so much information all at once, it wasn't clear what she was asking my viewpoint on. I turned to Mr. Johnson and asked him to give me his interpretation of the question. He laughed out loud and said, "I haven't a clue what she is talking about or what she wants you to respond to. I don't listen to her when she rambles. Communication is our main problem. That's why we're here."

In less than twenty minutes, the Johnsons had violated at least ten principles of effective communication. As she spoke, he sighed, grunted, rolled his eyes, and mumbled sarcastic remarks under his breath. The Johnsons had several issues that needed to be addressed, but all of them required improved communications between the two of them. Although both the speaker (Mrs. Johnson) and the listener (Mr. Johnson) were at fault, it is likely they will shift the blame.

Effective communication in marriage begins with the individual. Each person must decide that they will do their part to improve the communication in the marriage. Doing your part means assessing your heart. It means surrendering to the Lord, renewing your mind, and controlling your tongue. These are but a few of the things that helped me as I dealt with my unbalanced relationship. I had to allow God to change the way I was communicating with my husband. So when you think about improving the communication in your marriage, think about yourself. It begins with you.

BLESS THE LORD AT ALL TIMES

"I will bless the LORD at all times: his praise shall continually be in my mouth" (Psalm 34:1 KJV). As believers in Christ, whether married or single, it is important that we bless the Lord at all times. It is not just the words that we say; it is the way that we carry ourselves and the way that we interact with each other. Communication is both verbal and nonverbal. It comprises many different things, all working together to give information or create an impression—our words, our thoughts, our attitudes, and our actions. Our entire being communicates, whether we plan to or not. Therefore, *everything* we do and say should bless the Lord.

Surrender to the Lord

I Will Bless Thee, Oh Lord!

I will bless thee, oh Lord.
I will bless thee, oh Lord.
With a heart of thanksgiving;
I will bless thee, oh Lord.

With my hands lifted up,
and my mouth filled praise.
With a heart of thanksgiving,
I will bless thee, oh Lord.

(Repeat from the top)

Figure 6-1

God is so awesome. Just think about the way He inspires us to be creative—the song, and ideas that He gives us to communicate. God gave me this picture the first time someone asked me to speak on communication. In preparation, I thought about how everything that we do should bless the Lord and how we should praise Him. So I drew a picture of a little character as an illustration of praise and used it to illustrate my point. Obviously, I am not an artist, but I drew the picture to accompany the words for the song, "I will bless Thee, Oh Lord." In the song the writer describes communication that blesses the Lord: a heart of thanksgiving, hands lifted up, and a mouth filled with praise.

Whenever I have a speaking engagement, I run some of my ideas past my husband and show him the information. When he looked at the little character, he kept asking, "Is that on communication?" I answered, "Yes. Don't you see the guy? He is blessing the Lord." My husband said, "That guy looks like he is under arrest." And I said, "Under arrest, huh?" Then I thought, "OK. I guess when you are under arrest they shout, 'Up against the wall. Throw your hands up.'"

When a policeman pulls a gun on you, you do not say, "Wait a minute. Don't shoot me." You raise your hands and get up against the wall. Similarly, we are under arrest to the Lord. When the Lord calls us, we should answer with our hands up, in surrender to Him. So the way this picture is drawn is not an accident. This little guy represents a person under arrest, surrendering to the Lord, saying, "Everything I do, Lord, I am going to do for You." He is ready to praise the Lord at all times, and he is a reminder that our communication should always bless the Lord.

Give Thanks

To bless the Lord, we must be thankful. "And whatever you do, whether in word or deed, do all in the name of the Lord Jesus, giving thanks to God the Father through Him" (Colossians 3:17 NIV). We are often ungrateful. We fail to take enough time to look with appreciation at the relationships and possessions that the Lord has blessed us with. If we are going to bless the Lord, we must remember to give thanks to God for the things He has done. We need to thank God for the people He has placed in our lives and for the opportunities that we have to communicate on His behalf. To communicate on the Lord's behalf involves more than just sharing with others what we think or how we feel. It also involves showing love and forgiveness, doing right, and extending mercy to others in gratitude to God who has done so much for us—more than we can ask or think.

Renew Your Mind

To bless the Lord, we must learn what pleases Him. "For my thoughts are not your thoughts, neither are your ways my ways, saith the Lord" (Isaiah 55:8 KJV). In order to bless the Lord and to bless other people, the Word of God must renew our minds. If you are not in the Word and applying the Word in your life, you are basically out there saying what you want to say, doing what you want to do, and hoping that the Lord will bless it in the process. That is not the way Christian communication works. This is often the way it goes, but effective Christian communication works when we "bless the Lord at all times." It works when we encourage, edify, and lift up others. We cannot do this without God's direction.

As we discussed my drawing of the guy praising the Lord, my husband continued, "Well, why does he have this big, empty forehead? The guy doesn't have any eyes. He doesn't have a nose, and there is no brain up there." I said, "Sure, there is a brain up there." Scripture says, "Let this mind be in you, which was also in Christ Jesus" (Philippians 2:5 KJV). Our minds must be renewed. Scripture tells us "to think on these things," then it gives us a whole list of things to think about. "Finally, brethren, whatsoever things are true, whatsoever things are honest, whatsoever things are just, whatsoever things are pure, whatsoever things are lovely, whatsoever things are of good report; if there be any virtue, and if there be any praise, think on these things" (Philippians 4:8 KJV). When we fill our mind with the things of Christ—His attitudes, actions, desires, His compassion and love for others—and we continuously think on the things in the Word, it will change our communication.

Pray for a Clean Heart

To bless the Lord, pray for a clean heart. "Create in me a clean heart, O God; and renew a right spirit within me" (Psalm 51:10 KJV). It is not enough to have our minds filled with Christ Jesus and praise flowing from our lips; we must also have a clean heart. The issues in our hearts affect the things that flow from our lips. Scripture teaches us that from the abundance of the heart the mouth speaks. "A good man out of the good treasure of his heart bringeth forth that which is good; and an evil man out of the evil treasure of his heart bringeth forth that which is evil: for of the abundance of the heart his mouth speaketh" (Luke 6:45 KJV). In fact, Proverbs 4:23 commands, "Keep thy heart with all diligence; for out of it are the issues of life" (KJV).

I often pray, "Create in me a clean heart, Lord." I know that whatever is in my heart will eventually come out of my mouth. If I have been thinking, "I don't know why I'm with him anyway," then that is what's going to come out. Or if I am always thinking, "He never does this; he never does that," as soon as I get an opportunity, that comment will flow from my mouth. I'm sure that you have noticed this in your own life. Many times you are not aware of how your thoughts influence your words. Then there are times you are just waiting for the opportunity to give him a "piece of your mind." But when you have a thankful mind and a grateful heart, whenever there is an opportunity to speak you will remember how God has blessed you, and you will bless the Lord in your communication. The key here is desire. You have to want to change your mind.

We cannot fool God. Psalm 139 talks about how the Lord knows us intimately: He knows our going out and our coming in, He knew us when we were created in our mothers' wombs, He knows every word on our lips before we speak it, and He knows every thought that we have before we think it. So we need to confess wrong thoughts, words, attitudes, and actions, and say to the Lord, "Let the words of my mouth, and the meditation of my heart, be acceptable in thy sight, O Lord, my strength, and my redeemer" (Psalm 19:14 KJV).

Now, look again at the drawing of the guy praising the Lord. Do you see the outline that represents his heart? This is a reminder that we should always pray that God will create in us a clean heart.

Control Your Tongue

To bless the Lord, we must watch what we say. "If anyone considers himself religious and yet does not keep a tight rein on his tongue, he deceives himself and his religion is worthless" (James 1:26 NIV). Controlling our words may be the most difficult thing we do. The task of control is made more daunting for women because we *use* so many more words than men. It has been estimated that women speak about 50,000 words a day to men's 25,000. Add anger and disgust to the equation and you have a tongue out of control. So this issue of controlling your tongue is serious. And please understand me, I know how difficult it can be to "bridle" this small member, but bridle it you must. Because once your word is out there—it's out there. And think about it, sometimes the harsh and thoughtless things we say can transform a mild argument into a major fight. I'm sure many of us could tell some stories about the number of arguments that could have been avoided if we had just been quiet.

This truth is important to remember, especially in an unequally yoked relationship. James 1:26 is not written to those who are spiritually mature or elders in the faith. It does not even say to do this if you are a good Christian or if you really know the Lord. It is written to anyone who merely considers himself or herself to be religious. There are a lot of unsaved people who consider themselves to be religious but have no relationship with the Lord whatsoever. In contrast, not only do we say we are religious, but we are Christians who know the Lord and have a personal relationship with Him. Therefore, it is extremely important that we, as Christians, watch what we say.

My husband had a list of all the things that good Christians should do, and keeping a tight rein on your tongue was one of them. When I got ready to say something, he would give me that "And you are a good Christian" look. I was reminded, at that point, that my communication was making my religion worthless. I had to be able to control my tongue to be an example to him.

Our accountability before God is another reason that we must control our tongues. "But I tell you that men will have to give account on the day of judgment for every careless word they have spoken. For by your words you will be acquitted, and by your words you will be condemned" (Matthew 12:36–37 NIV). We ought to get scared just thinking about that. If we consider some of the things we say in light of God's holiness and judgment, we would understand more clearly why we should be praying for forgiveness, going before the Lord confessing our sins, and asking the Lord to give us a clean heart.

When we confess sinful speech and begin to say those things that please the Lord, we can smile like the little guy "under arrest" in the drawing. We can say, "Lord, I surrender my entire being. I am surrendering my mind, my heart, my lips, all of me, to the right communication process that I may do and say something that is pleasing to You."

Steps to Good Communication

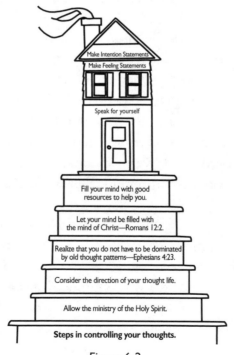

Figure 6-2

As we surrender to the Lord, give thanks to God in everything, constantly renew our mind with the Word, pray for a clean heart, and watch what we say, our communication will bless the Lord.

STEPS TO GOOD COMMUNICATION

Consider the Direction of Your Thoughts

Another key to good communication is to consider the direction of your thoughts. *Consider* is a key word; self-awareness and insight is a good thing. We must become sensitive to what is going on inside us and more aware of our thought processes. In other words, we must know what we are thinking and then do something about it. We must ask ourselves, "If I keep thinking this way, where will it lead me?" What are the things that you constantly think about?

God's Word gives us a whole list of things to think about: "Finally, brethren, whatsoever things are true, whatsoever things are honest, whatsoever things are just, whatsoever things are pure, whatsoever things are lovely, whatsoever things are of good report; if there be any virtue, and if there be any praise, think on these things" (Philippians 4:8 KJV). When I began to think differently about my husband and my marriage, I began to say things that brought peace to my heart, in my mind, and in my home. Challenge yourself today to think about those things that are pure and lovely and of good report. Notice the change in your actions.

Realize that You Can Change Your Mind

Thinking is a process of putting off one thing, or changing your mind about it, and putting on something different. You can put off negative thinking, renew your mind with the Word of God, and put on positive thinking. You do not have to be dominated by old habits or thought patterns. Scripture says that we must take every thought into captivity. "Casting down imaginations, and every high thing that exalteth itself against the knowledge of God, and bringing into captivity every thought to the obedience of Christ" (2 Corinthians 10:5 KJV). If you feel yourself wandering off, stop your train of thought and pull yourself back in. If you know that your mind is veering to the left, then you need to bring it back to the right. You can stay on track by prayerfully considering the direction of your thought life.

You can also reframe the way you look at things. In counseling, I meet women whose unsaved husbands no longer want to spend time at home, basically because their wives play praise music all the time. These men are always hearing "Praise the Lord," "Hallelujah," "God bless you," "God is good"—church talk or what many have called "Christianese"—and their wives know all the terminology, but their lifestyles are often contradictory. Frankly, this talk is a turn-off to the unsaved and carnal-minded. It wouldn't be a bad idea to save the "Christianese" for those folks at church, especially when your actions aren't quite lining up with your lingo.

Some men even work long hours on the job simply because they would rather be anywhere but home. Usually their wives find this situation to be very negative. They often complain about their husband's absence and lack of attention. However, they fail to see the inconsistency in greeting him at the door with the praise music playing in the background while they nag and fuss and complain, "You are never at home. Why are you working all the time?" This behavior gives the husband even more reason to avoid spending time at home with his wife. (I'm telling you what I know.)

When I counsel women in unbalanced relationships, we work together to change the way they look at things. I ask, "What good things can you say about someone who works all the time?" Then together we begin to list some things: "He is faithful. He is committed. He is diligent. He brings his money home. He puts food on the table and a roof over your head." The goal is to try to put things in a more positive light so that she can respond to him in a positive manner when he does come home. After we make the list, the goal is to "think on these things."

Fill Your Mind with Good Resources

Remember, if you are always watching TV talk shows and foolish sitcoms, then those are the things you will find yourself talking about because they are on your mind. If you are reading the miscellaneous magazines with the gossip about who is doing what with whom, the places people have gone, or the latest fashions, then those are the things that will eventually come out.

We must fill our minds with good resources. Many good books have been written on the subject of communication. The companion Bible Study Workbook contains a list of excellent books that are written from a biblical perspective. However, the Bible is the very best source of information. If you never read another book, read your Bible on a daily basis. In it, God has given us all things that pertain to life and godliness. "According as his divine power hath given unto us all things that pertain unto life and godliness, through the knowledge of him that hath called us to glory and virtue" (2 Peter 1:3 KJV).

Spend Time with the Lord

One of the most important things that we can do to ensure good communication is to spend time with the Lord. We are changed in His presence. If we are not in the presence of the Lord, every day that we go without spending time with Him, we revert more and more to the way we used to be and the way we used to act. To be transformed into His image, we must spend time with Him.

Question: Have you spent time with the Lord today? Here is a simple rule to remember: If you have not spent time with the Lord, you are not fit to spend time with anybody else.

Allow the Ministry of the Holy Spirit

Sometimes we struggle with knowing what to say. Therefore, we must allow the ministry of the Holy Spirit to operate in and through us. God already knows that we don't know what we are supposed to say. That is why we need to keep a tight rein on our tongues. Until we know that what we're getting ready to say is of God, we should not say anything.

Some people say, "I am not a talker. That is not my style; I am more of an introvert. I'm not sure what to say half the time. I like to just think things through and really get it right before I say anything at all." In Exodus 4:10–12, we find Moses saying, "I don't know what to say. You're going to send me to talk to somebody?" (paraphrased). Similarly, you know that God has sent you to talk to your spouse, your children, your coworkers, or your friends. You know you need to go and speak to them, but you don't go. Instead you say to God, "Lord, You know I don't know what to say." And you just don't say anything. Or you know there is something you could say to edify someone else, but you can't figure out how to put it into words. So you think, "Oh, maybe somebody else will say something to make him feel better." Or you know somebody that needs correcting in a certain situation, instruction, or direction and you want to speak to them, but you are not sure what to say. So you tell yourself, "Well, somebody will tell her."

God gave us our mouths; He knows exactly what we need to say. Basically, when we go in obedience to God's direction, all we need to do is open our mouths and allow the Lord to speak through us. Do not go in with a preplanned agenda thinking, "I am going to say this, this, this, and this." Go in and allow the ministry of the Holy Spirit to work, because the Lord knows what needs to be said.

In 1 Corinthians 2:1-4, Paul says, "When I came to you, brothers, I did not come with eloquence or superior wisdom as I proclaimed to you the testimony about God. . . . I came to you in weakness and fear, and with much trembling. My message and my preaching were not with wise and persuasive words, but with a demonstration of the Spirit's power" (NIV). Even when you have to talk with people who are well educated, highly intellectual, or experts in this or that, do not be intimidated. To communicate appropriately, we must realize that it is going to be the ministry of the Holy Spirit working in and through us. He will help us to say what we need to say. It's nice if we possess great intellect, deep wisdom, and an extensive vocabulary, but it is the ministry of the Holy Spirit that will make our communication truly effective.

Levels of Communication

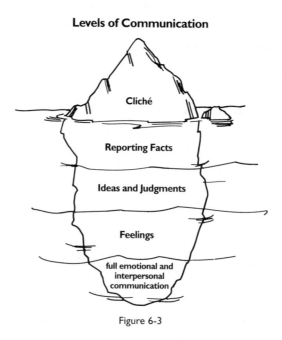

Figure 6-3

LEVELS OF COMMUNICATION

A goal of good marital communication is to experience the depths of full emotional interpersonal communication.

This picture of an iceberg in water illustrates five levels of communication. Above the water, just the tip of the iceberg is visible.

Speaking in clichés represents just the tip of the iceberg. Clichés are commonplace statements like, "Let's have lunch." Now, how many people who make this statement actually call you for an appointment in a couple of days? Probably very few people follow through. Clichés are slogans that substitute for genuine communication; it's the polite thing to say.

The next level is *reporting the facts*. We often find that men are very good about reporting the facts. The facts are the actual reality concerning what happened. "It was eighty degrees outside." No question about it, that is a fact. If you say it was hot outside, hot is a matter of perception. It was hot to you, but it felt wonderful to me. However, if you state that it was eighty degrees, no one can argue with that. It is measurable, and it is a fact. The statement "I had a flat tire" is also a statement of fact. However, a statement of fact may be incomplete. For example, "I was embarrassed about the fact that I had a flat tire when three people I knew drove by" communicates a completely different message.

Sharing ideas and judgment requires an exchange of personal information. When you start talking about ideas and judgment, you are communicating your thoughts and opinions, your impressions about certain things, or your conclusions with someone else.

The next level of communication is *reporting feelings*. Have you ever been in a situation where you knew that someone was upset, but you had no clue why? You had no idea what the person was upset about; you just knew he or she was upset, angry, or frightened. Usually, women are better at reporting their feelings. We may fail to articulate why something happened or identify the reasons behind what is going on, but we tell how we feel about it. We often skip the other levels of communication to report our emotions, sensations, and intuition about certain things. Our beliefs and attitudes are also frequently communicated in feeling statements.

At the bottom, we find the deepest level of communication: *full emotional interpersonal communication*. It has become easy for most people to use clichés, talk about their ideas and judgments, relate the facts, and even discuss their feelings. But to have full interpersonal communication requires a level of transparency that a lot of people do not want to get into. We are not sure that we want others to know us that well. If they do, they might decide that they do not like what they know. So we tend to guard ourselves. This is true even within the marriage relationship. However, if we really want to communicate intimately and effectively with those we claim to be close to, then we must learn to venture into this deeper level.

PRACTICAL POINTS OF INTERPERSONAL COMMUNICATION

Effective communication is a continual learning process. We all need to make a habit of applying the practical points of interpersonal communication.

Speak for Yourself

Speak for yourself; do not say what the other person is thinking or put words in the other person's mouth. Do not say, "You always . . ." or "You did . . ." If we would use more personal or "I" statements, communication would go a lot smoother. It is a lot easier to let the other person own their part of the conversation than to have to take complete ownership and responsibility. The key is to avoid blaming, projecting, and mind reading. Yeah, you know him or her, but you cannot read his or her mind, so stop telling your mate what they were going to say! Because you don't know—just listen.

If the person takes a little bit longer to say certain things, give them the time they need to say it. When you fill in the blanks, you may come up with the wrong answer. Then instead of arguing the point, they may say, "Yeah, OK," because they know right away you aren't listening; you aren't giving them a chance to share what is on their heart. If you have already come to your own conclusions without the facts, what's the point of conversation? So they say, "OK," and mentally walk away. And you think you know what they were talking about. Instead, learn to speak for yourself. Simply communicate your wants, your desires, your needs, and your intentions. Do not cloud the communications process.

Discuss Your Feelings

Good communication requires that we become sensitive. We must develop the ability to communicate our own feelings and to notice the feelings and address the needs of others. To do this we must be able to discuss feelings and learn to make feeling statements. Many people find it is easier to communicate positive emotions such as excitement, happiness, surprise, or elation. However, it is just as important to let your spouse know when you are sad, frustrated, or disappointed.

Reveal Your Intentions

Our conversation usually has an unstated purpose. We fail to make intention statements: "The reason I am saying what I am saying is because . . ." For example, a husband comes home from work and his wife says, "You never kiss me when you come in." This is not a personal statement, it is not a feeling statement, and it is not an intention statement. Her intent was to get a kiss. Can you think of a better way to get a kiss than to say, "You never kiss me anymore"? A better approach would be to say, "Give me a kiss." That is very straightforward, but saying "give me" puts responsibility and pressure on the other person. She could also say, "I would like a kiss." Her husband could still respond to her by saying, "I don't want to kiss you today." But by speaking for herself, communicating her feelings, and revealing her intentions, she can reduce the possibility of misunderstanding or confusion.

Say What You Mean

It is amazing how simple communication can become when we say what we mean and mean what we say. But that is not what we do. Sometimes, we simply fail to choose our words carefully, and though we mean to say one thing, we actually say something else. Too often, we say one thing, then we expect the other person to guess what we meant to say. We do not tell them exactly what we want, but we expect them to guess what it is. In doing so, we confuse and trap others in our communication process. It is like thinking, "See if you can guess what I mean; and if you can't guess, I'm going to be upset about it." It's like saying, "Read my mind."

While I have tried for a long time, I just haven't mastered the art of mind reading. I work on it; I am very good at finishing other people's sentences. When they are taking too long, sometimes I will put words in their mouth and hope that they are right. But, trust me, this just does not promote effective communication. Sometimes the best thing to do when we can't get it right is to be quiet.

We must become aware of what we are communicating to others and think about the responses we receive. We should ask ourselves, "Did the person understand my message? Did it have the impact that I expected? Did I get the results or response that I wanted? And if not, why not?" When we speak for ourselves, say things that reflect our feelings, acknowledge the feelings of others, reveal our intentions, and say what we mean, it makes the communication process a lot easier.

Understand the Communication Process

Whenever we speak, we are actually sending coded messages. A simple textbook model of communication defines three basic processes: encode a message, send/receive it, and decode it. The speaker is the encoder or the person who is sending the message.

He has something on his mind or in his heart that he wants to communicate to somebody else. He turns the message into a code by determining the words, actions, tone of voice, etc., he will use to send the message. The person who receives it has to decode or decide how to interpret the message.

Let us look again at the example of the wife who says to her husband, "You never kiss me anymore." She is sending the message "You never kiss me." Those are the words that she decides to use. Her husband may decode the message as "She is mad because I did not kiss her again." That may not be the message she intended to send, but because of the way she encoded her message (both verbally and nonverbally), or the way that he decoded it, her husband received an angry or complaining message. He responds, "As soon as I come in, you start complaining. Now you say that I never kiss you anymore. Well, I am tired when I come in, and I didn't think you wanted to be close to me." Now they have a fight on their hands; they are both going back and forth in heated conversation.

This is how miscommunication in marriage often occurs. When we send the message, we don't send what we intend to communicate and the other person doesn't have a clue about what we are saying, so they send back something different.

For instance, I could ask you to draw a kitchen appliance. Then, when I saw your drawing, I could complain and ask, "Why didn't you draw a mixer? That is what I meant for you to draw. Hmm, how did you miss that?" Or what if I said, "Go to the store and buy a loaf of bread." What would you buy? In other words, if you go the store and get a loaf of bread, what type of bread would you buy? I'm sure not everyone would go to the store and buy Butter Crest wheat bread for $1.39, right? Butter Crest is the only brand of wheat bread that I eat. Can you imagine how many varieties of bread I would end up with if I asked that question of ten people?

Confusion—that is what happens between people when they don't communicate clearly. I may be thinking Butter Crest wheat bread at $1.39, but that is not what I said. My instructions were to "Go buy bread." So a person would go and buy the loaf of bread and come back with the wrong bread (according to me). Now we have a debate: "Why didn't you buy what you know I like?" "Why didn't you tell me what to buy? You knew exactly what you wanted." "We have been living together nine years. Why don't you know I only eat Butter Crest?" "But that is not what you asked for." And on it goes.

Too often the problem starts here: We have in mind what we want, but we fail to communicate it. What we think and what we say are not always the same thing. But we still expect the person we are talking to on the other end to understand. Instead of saying, "You did it wrong," we should think, "Maybe I sent the wrong message." First determine whether you sent the message clearly. If you said, "Go get a loaf of bread," and the person comes back with a loaf of plain white bread, just eat it. Don't talk about what you wanted, what you meant, or what they should have done. You blew it; smile, thank him or her, and eat the bread.

Speak Specifically

Good communication is specific. We need to clearly state what we are thinking and what it is we want to achieve. Sometimes, instead of being specific about what we want, we ask the other person to tell us what they think, hoping that what they think is what we want. In doing so, we make statements or ask questions that bait or trap people, and miscommunication and misunderstanding is the result.

For example, instead of asking, "What did you think about the sermon this morning?" we make leading statements or questions like, "Didn't you think that was a great sermon this morning?" Then, if the person does not agree that it was a great sermon, the conversation is set for an argument.

If you really want to discuss how much you enjoyed the sermon, you could simply make a personal statement: "I thought it was a great sermon." If you want to know what someone else thought, you should ask: "What did you think about the sermon?" It is very important that we listen to ourselves and evaluate what we are saying. We want to be sure we are not baiting others, or trapping them, or giving them leading statements in the course of conversation.

Get to the Point

I am known for my lead-ins; most of my friends know that whenever I begin to tell a story, the first thing I say is, "Let me give you my intro." When they say, "Sabrina, I do not have time for all of that. What do you want to tell me? I've got five minutes," I reprocess by thinking, "What can I tell you in five minutes?" I may have to say, "Well, let me call you later," because I know that my story will take more than five minutes.

When I call them, I say, "Now, let me tell you this, but let me give you the intro first." The introduction is the peripheral kind of stuff that really is not relevant, like who was wearing what, what the temperature was, or how I got there.

Recently, I was sharing a story with a friend of mine. But as I began to set the stage and work my way up to the climax, she said, "How does it end? Is it a positive or negative outcome?" After talking about all of the other things that happened in the process, it may be some time later before I actually arrive at the point (although everything leading up to it will be relevant).

This is often how women communicate. We rush in, and we start talking about lots of different things at once, with thoughts and perceptions going back and forth. The person who is listening is wondering, "OK, what is the point of all of this?" and wishing that we would get to the point or be quiet. So they lose interest; they really do not care how the story ends because we lost them a long time ago.

We are saying something that we think is very important, but we are giving too much information. When we talk about too many things all at once, it is hard for the listener to figure out what is most important and what they are supposed to be paying attention to. If you know there is something specific you want the person to understand, say that part and leave out all of the extraneous stuff. Let the person know what is important and what is extra.

In the context of a marriage relationship, imagine a wife telling her husband about her day. She talks about the kids, what she did all day long, her job, what she watched on TV, the laundry, the bills that need to be paid, etc. While listening, he wonders, "Now, what am I supposed to remember? What do you want me to do? What is it that you want me to know?" and he is not sure what to think. She is trying to paint a picture of how harried her day was, hoping that her husband will understand that she needs to be comforted. Then when he does not understand, she is upset. She goes away angry, and he is wondering what is wrong. Now they are playing mind games, simply because of poor communication.

Instead of saying, "And this happened, and that happened . . ." when you are frustrated, say you are frustrated. If there was too much going on and you want a hug, you need some affection, you need attention, you need to be comforted because you had a long, hard day—say that. We can avoid some communication problems by simply getting to the point.

Ask Yourself: Is It Relevant?

We must evaluate what we are communicating to others. Sometimes our conversation has no point. It is not relevant; we are just talking about miscellaneous stuff. However, Scripture says that "the heart of the righteous weighs its answers" and "a wise man's heart guides his mouth, and his lips promote instruction" (Proverbs 15:28; 16:23 NIV).

Listen to Others

It almost goes without saying that when people are talking to you, you should be listening—not just hearing, but also giving your attention. "Wherefore, my beloved brethren, let every man be swift to hear, slow to speak, slow to wrath" (James 1:19 KJV). Communication is a circular process. We send and receive messages; we speak and we listen. Good communication requires listening.

Adapt to Each Other

You should not try to change anyone other than yourself. Unfortunately, that is often one of the first things that happens in a marriage. Before you get married, you say, "I don't particularly like this or that, but it's cool; I can live with it." Then you get married and you say, "I am not going to take it. You have got to change." You try to make a square peg fit into a round hole.

God has made each of us unique. We are all "fearfully and wonderfully made" (Psalm 139:14 KJV). We must not try to change people. We need to learn to love them the way that they are, and for who they are. If we learn how to adapt our personalities to one another, we can encourage each other, edify one another, and live together in peace. It can be done—not by changing the other person, but by understanding who they are, considering the way that they think, and then working with them to discover the best way to communicate.

Early in my marriage, when my husband would come home from work, the first thing I would want to do is talk. I would want to know, "How was your day? What did you do? What happened? How did you feel?" But when he came in from work, all he wanted to do was sit down, be by himself, and watch James Bond. He wanted to unwind. He has an entire James Bond collection, and he has seen every movie at least twenty times. I personally do not understand the concept, but I know it's what he likes, so I have to respect that.

At first, this was always a point of contention and conflict. My husband would come in and I would rush up to him and want to hug and kiss and talk. And he would communicate nonverbally, "Back off, give me space. Give me some room here first." I spent many frustrated evenings wondering what I was doing wrong, while he came home from work and went to the basement with a video-tape.

We argued about that for a long time. I can be very clear about what I want, and I like to get what I want. So at first I was insistent on trying to change the situation. When it wasn't working, I sub-mitted to the Lord and prayed, "Lord, help me to understand him better. Show me how to do this better." Finally, it sunk in: "OK, I can't change him. It is not my role or my responsibility." When I stopped trying to change him and tried to understand him more, things changed—not him. Because changing him was no longer the goal.

Eventually, I realized I needed to respect his space. I thought, "Scripture says, dwell with your spouse according to knowledge. I know the man likes his space when he comes home from work. Why do I insist on invading his space when he comes in? If I am dwelling according to knowledge, I know some basic things. He wants to be left alone." I had a choice. I could have turned away from him and spent a lot of time being upset, thinking all of the wrong thoughts. I could have thought, "Why doesn't he want to talk to me? Maybe I'm just not that interesting. Maybe he's more interested in his job." But I finally realized that the point was that he had a long, hard, tiring day, and he wanted to unwind alone. Giving him his space meant he had time to shake off the frustration of his day.

When I started dwelling according to knowledge, life became a lot easier for both of us. I began to respect his individual needs and aspects of his personality. Now, when he comes in, I say, "Hey," and give him a hug and a kiss. Then I go left, and he goes right. He unwinds; then later we get together and laugh and talk. It works wonderfully. But I had to choose not to try to change him; I had to give him his space, understand how he processes things, and live with that.

Understand the Importance of Timing

It is also good to know how much time you have to communicate a message effectively. I can get very involved in conversation, but my husband likes to talk in short spurts at a time. He is thinking, "A fifteen-minute conversation is really too long already. But I will give you fifteen minutes, and then I need a break." So I would have to think in fifteen-minute segments. And since I can talk for hours, I am thinking, "I have all of this stuff I want to tell you about. Do I want to tell all fifteen stories, a minute each? Or, do I want to get two stories in and get a good seven minutes for each, and then come back to the other thirteen stories later on?" So I have to think about it.

I don't try to convince him to talk longer. Once he sits past fifteen minutes, he is not listening anyway. He is off somewhere else, thinking about all of the other stuff he wanted to be doing, and he is wondering, "How long is this going to take?" He is no longer processing or hearing what I'm saying. So I deal with the fifteen-minute blocks by prioritizing. I decide, "OK, this is the most important thing that I want to talk about, now that I have your attention for fifteen minutes." And I go for it; he sits, he participates, he laughs, he asks questions, and he gets involved in the conversation. Then we take a break, and I wait for my next fifteen-minute segment. I know what else I want to talk about, but I wait. Considering his time limits helps me to stay focused and not go here and there in conversation.

We must accept some things about other people. For example, I know that I have to skip the introductions with my husband. (My friends are a bit more tolerant.) I know that in conversation with my husband I have fifteen minutes to communicate, so I decide exactly what I want to talk about. If I just start talking, he may hear some of the details but have no clue about what I really wanted to discuss with him because I have lost him by going past his time limit.

In contrast, whenever he talks with me, I want to know all the details, not just a sound bite. So I say, "Honey, let's schedule a time to continue our conversation so we can discuss all of the other stuff I want to know and I can ask questions about what else happened." I have learned to understand the importance of timing.

Now, our issues are not yours. Think about your mate. What irritates her or him about your style of communication? What changes in your storytelling style would he or she appreciate? Listen, but more importantly, watch his or her reactions to you when you talk. Then ask direct questions about your impressions.

Let's pray.

> *Dear Lord, Communication is a gift from You. It's an opportunity to share a part of ourselves so that others may see Your glory in us. Renew our minds so that we see communication as You do. Help us to meditate on things of virtue and praise so that our communication builds each other up and never tears each other down. Teach us, more than anything else, to communicate in love as we consider our spouses and dwell with them according to knowledge. In Jesus' name we pray. Amen.*

Prayer Requests
Mike and study for weekend
James allergies
Jobs for Roger.
Mathew Tina's son

Next week @ cove

CHAPTER SEVEN

Friends:
Yours, Mine,
and Ours

F riends—almost everyone has them. You have heard the saying: "Let's all be friends." There are so many different songs about friends, poems about friends, and books about friends. In fact, there is an abundance of information on friends and friendly relationships. However, there is relatively little information about how your friends affect your marriage. My friends and José's friends had both a positive and negative affect on our marriage relationship, yet God taught me many lessons through those relationships.

DEFINITIONS OF FRIENDSHIP

First, let's begin with some basic information. Remember, it's the basics that we all need to grab hold of and embrace. We talk about friends all the time, but what is a friend? As you read the definitions below, think about your own personal relationships.

■ *A friend is someone who enjoys being around you and accepts you for who you are, even when things are bad.* No one is perfect. If we are honest, we must admit that everything about us is not always great and wonderful. Everyone has idiosyncrasies—little habits that get on other people's nerves. But a friend is someone who knows you and accepts you as you are.

■ *A friend is someone who knows you well and likes you anyway.* Scripture says that we can be confident "that he which hath begun a good work in you will perform it until the day of Jesus Christ" (Philippians 1:6b KJV). The Lord will be working on us until the day of completion. There is always room for improvement; there is always something more about ourselves we need to work on. But a friend likes us anyway. He or she realizes that we are a work in progress; we are a masterpiece in development. "For we are his workmanship, created in Christ Jesus unto good works, which God hath before ordained that we should walk in them" (Ephesians 2:10 KJV). A friend can see the character of Christ that is being formed in us. Think of the people in your life who often tell you, "You can do that." "I believe in you." "You know, I can tell that you are a woman of integrity." "I can see that you love the Lord." A friend is a person who can see the best in you.

■ *A friend is someone who knows you intimately and is committed to your best under all circumstances, regardless of the risks to the relationship.* To be committed to your best interest is really a matter of being committed to seeing God's best for you. Sometimes, that means that a friend will have to tell you some things that you don't want to hear. Or, it may be necessary for you to say some things that your friend may not want to hear. But a friend is someone who will speak the truth in love. Anyone can tell you something nice. But a friend is willing to take the risk to tell you what you need to hear—to tell you what "thus saith the

Lord," whether you want to hear it or not. Proverbs 27:6 says, "Faithful are the wounds of a friend; but the kisses of an enemy are deceitful" (KJV). A friend who is committed to God's best for you is willing to say, "I see some things that you need to be aware of. Therefore, it is my responsibility before the Lord as your friend to share those things with you."

■ *A friend is a trusted confidant to whom you are mutually drawn as a companion, who loves you not for your performance, and whose influence draws you closer to Christ.* Scripture talks about "fickle friends" (Job 16:20; 19:19; Psalm 38:11; Matthew 26:56; Luke 15:12–15; John 16:32; 2 Timothy 1:15; 4:10). "Fickle friends" are people who love you when you have a pocketful of money or who want to be around you only when things are going well. They like you because of what you can do for them, because you are talented or athletic, because you are an eloquent speaker or singer, or because you have a particular job, drive an expensive car, live in a certain neighborhood, etc. In other words, it's your possessions or performance that they like. When these things disappear, so do these so-called "friends." But a real friend will stick by you no matter what.

A friend is someone who challenges you and encourages you to grow spiritually. If you have a relationship where all you do is share jokes and kind words and you never see anything wrong with each other or never have anything to say to help each other to grow spiritually, it may just be a cover-up. Loving confrontation between friends causes us to lay aside our masks. Proverbs 27:17 says, "Iron sharpeneth iron; so a man sharpeneth the countenance of his friend" (KJV). The phrase "iron sharpens iron" refers to a friend who can counsel you according to God's Word. So when you think about your friends, ask yourself: Does this friendship cause both my friend and me to draw closer to God?

SHARING MY STRUGGLES

My husband and I are very good friends. However, this is a relatively new development. We have come full circle. We started out as friends when we first met and our relationship deepened in the first year of marriage. But after I became a Christian, it was like sleeping with the enemy for both of us. Before we were married, we knew many good things about each other. (Whenever you are ministering to single women, encourage them to become friends before they become marriage partners. You definitely want to know the man you are marrying.) I knew that he was tall, he was good-looking, and he had a great job—keep in mind that I was not a Christian when I married and neither was he, so all the things that I was excited about were worldly things. I did not look for spiritual value because that was not a primary focus. I did know that he was a good man. He was fun-loving and carefree. He was kind-hearted and generous. These were all admirable traits that encouraged me.

During our first year of marriage, we spent a lot of time hanging out and meeting other people. We had many friends who were couples, and we participated in activities and went on trips together. We were always entertaining, having a party, or going to a party. It was one party after another—a very draining lifestyle to say the least. Of course, I did not think that at the time.

When I accepted Christ, everything changed. Then, it seemed like all of the things that excited me upset him. And whenever he wanted to bring his friends home, I would think, "Not those heathens. They talk loud. They curse like sailors. They want to smoke and drink in the house." We argued frequently about our friends, our activities with them, and how they would or would not affect us. When I considered his friends and their vices, what concerned me the most was that all of his friends also wanted him to go out, and that meant that he would behave the way they did. (OK, the way I did before I became a Christian.) They wanted things to be as they

156

used to be. We almost divorced because of disagreements over what our friends had to say about our marriage and what they thought we should be doing. Finally, I learned that I had to put my husband in the Lord's hands (and get there myself).

I spent much of our second year of marriage at home in tears, while every weekend my husband was off with his friends. He was having a wonderful time. And I was at home thinking, "Woe is me. My husband doesn't love me. All the other women are out with their husbands going to couple's events together, and I have been left here alone. Woe is me." I understood later that this was not the case. Not everybody was at home with his or her spouse cuddled in front of a fireplace or out together having a wonderful time. There were many other Christian women alone at home too. I found out who they were, and we all started spending time together. (It was a great idea, an instant support system!)

For the next three or four years, both my husband and I desperately wanted to be good friends—to become best friends. But we were always passing back and forth, and we were never working on our relationship at the same time. At first, I was the one who really wanted to work on the marriage, and he was out with his friends. Then, by the time I accepted the fact that he was not coming home to spend time with me and I had learned to get together with my friends, he came home. Our roles reversed. I was always leaving, and he would be at home saying, "Well, when are you coming back?" I would reply, "We are going to the show, and then we are going out to dinner. I will be home by eleven o'clock." Then I would think, "What is the problem?" I had learned to make plans as a defense mechanism, but I also understood it was exacerbating the conflict in our marriage.

We became bitter. My husband felt like my friends were my first priority because while he was at home wanting to spend time with me, I was out with the girls. Then, when I finally decided to stay home, I kept saying, "Well, let's plan something for the weekend."

And his response would always be, "Don't you have plans already?" I had set a precedent because I always had plans that did not include him. It didn't matter that he had done the same thing first—created a world that excluded me.

I also spent a lot of time at church. I had many friends at church, and I was on entirely too many committees. My caution to married women who are involved in more than two or three church ministries, committees, activities, or groups is: Stop it. You don't have time for that many activities. You really do not. If you're trying to build a marriage, you just don't have time to be on the usher board, sing in the choir, and work in the church ministries. All of those things require a great deal of time, prayer, and preparation. Remember that God has also called you to a home ministry. If you have a spouse who doesn't know the Lord, you should be a living example of Christ's love before him. You cannot be a godly example at home if you are always at church.

My husband grew to resent the church because it was where I spent all of my happy moments. I would go off to church and I would come back home exhausted with all of my energy expended at church. After that, why would he want to be around me? I was so pitiful by the time I got home, I didn't want to be around myself!

When I finally came home and started to give my husband five or ten minutes of my time, the phone would start ringing. Of course, I had to talk to the caller about everything that happened at the church meeting. Then someone else would call and give me their impression of what happened. And the president of this committee would call to see if I would be at the meeting tomorrow and have the report ready. So I would spend the next hour or so after coming home from church on the phone with my friends.

Needless to say, my husband was not a happy person. He was very calm about it; he never really said anything. So for a long time

I didn't know that it bothered him. I just figured, "He doesn't care. You know, he has his own world. He's doing his own thing, and it's OK." I found out later, after I had changed, that my behavior was a problem for him. I also found out that he did not like several of my friends. Not because of their character or personality but because he felt they showed a lack of respect for him. He kept thinking, "You have had her for three hours; why do you have to call her now? Can I have her for five minutes?"

Take time to see where you fit in your spouse's life by answering the following personal questions:

- *How much time are you spending out with other people?*
- *How much time do you spend on the telephone?*
- *How much time do you spend with your husband/wife?*

EVALUATING YOUR FRIENDSHIPS

Carefully consider who your friends are. With whom are you sharing the things that are going on in your marriage? Why are you sharing the things that are going on in your marriage? What kind of character do these friends have?

Years ago, one of my friends said something I have always considered to be very special. I called her and tried to engage her in conversation, and she said, "You know, Sabrina, I really can't talk right now." And I asked, "Why not? What's going on?" She simply said, "Sabrina, let me call you back." But I kept thinking, "Is there a problem? Do you need help? Can I intervene?" Finally, she said, "I haven't spent time with the Lord yet. And because I haven't spent time with Him, I'm not fit to spend time with you." I thought, "Wow, that is kind of deep. She hasn't spent time with Him, so she can't even talk to me." I told her, "You know, after we get off the phone you can go have quiet time." But she answered, "No, my time of devotion with God is of utmost importance. Spending time with Him is critical." My friend is right. If we haven't spent time with the Lord, we aren't fit to spend time with anyone else.

If we are filled with the world, that is what we will share with other people. We will share the knowledge of the world. We will share what we read in the paper, what we see on TV, or what someone has recently shared with us. But when we have been in the presence of God, that is what we will share with others. We will share the knowledge of God, the wisdom of God, and the character of God.

Make sure your friend is someone who is concerned about godly things—a person who knows the Word of God and will turn to it when you call. Always keep in mind that friends are people who should draw you closer to God. Therefore, if they are telling you something that is contrary to the Word, then they are not really your friends.

I have a couple of friends who have been very positive influences in my life. When I was struggling in my marriage, I could go talk to and pray with them. They would never let me give details about the situation. In retrospect, I can appreciate their wisdom. At that point, I just wanted to unload and they understood that. They would ask me, "How did you respond?" I would think, "Let me tell you what he did to me first!" But they did not want to hear all the details. They were concerned about my response and whether it was a godly response. Did I still reflect Christ, even in my anger? Did I handle things appropriately?

Having friends who will turn you to the Word of God will make a difference in your life. Not friends who will just let you go on and on and rant and rave about all your problems—instead, you want friends you can turn to who will open the Word and find the appropriate Scripture.

One thing that I always caution women against is telling their friends their husband's faults. Other people will remember his faults long after you have forgotten them. Usually you want to tell somebody your husband's faults because you're angry and upset. But that is the time to turn to the Lord.

So whenever you find yourself wanting to call a friend and say, "This man . . ." and go on and on and on, take a deep breath and go before the Lord instead. He is the One you need to talk to.

When you think about your closest friends, ask yourself:

- *Are these people building a hedge around my marriage?*

- *How concerned are they about godly things?*

- *Or, are they the types who say, "Well, I never really liked him anyway," or "You know, I didn't like it when he did this the other day," or "I don't believe you put up with that!"?*

I have discovered over the years that I can put up with a whole lot more than most of my friends can because he is my husband and I want to keep him. When you join together as man and wife, there must be a commitment from day one that no matter what happens, you plan to stay together. Sometimes, the struggle is so great that you may wonder: "Will I make it?" "Is this worth it?" "Should I stay in this relationship?" But if you really believe the Lord and His Word, you know that He is working and He is using your relationship with your spouse to challenge you to grow and become more like Christ.

LEVELS OF FRIENDSHIP

I have always been a very friendly person. When I was growing up, I used to think that I had so many friends. I felt like I was a friend of everyone in the world. However, those people weren't all friends. They weren't people I could call on in a time of need. They were just people that I knew, people I had met at different points in life. The following diagram illustrates four different levels of friendship.

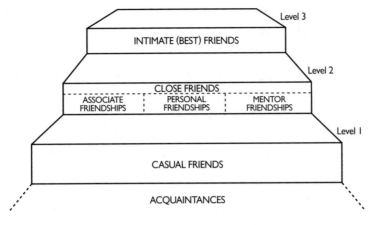

Figure 7-1

Friends and Friendship: The secrets of Drawing Closer by Jerry and Mary White. NavPress Singapore (exclusively available in the U.S. through Castle Bookstore, The Navigators, P.O. Box 6819, Colorado Springs, CO 80934, 719.272.7410, castlebookstore@navigators.com)

▪ *Acquaintances*

We cannot be friends with the world; we can simply know a lot of people without developing friendships with them. Statistics show that we can have anywhere from five hundred to twenty-five hundred acquaintances, based on the number of people we come into contact with each day. Just think about the people you see at the mall or the market, in the bank, on the job, on the city bus, or at your children's school. These people are acquaintances—people whom you see often in passing.

▪ *Casual Friends*

Casual friends are people you know by name and you see regularly. Statistics show that you can have up to fifty to one hundred casual friends. They are the people who serve with you on committees or who work with you on the job. In contrast, the people you see when you walk into the building at work are acquaintances, but the people who actually work with you can usually be considered casual friends.

162

■ *Close Friends*

Close friends are people who know more about you than just your name. They know some of your goals and aspirations, your beliefs and interests, or your desires and preferences. Believe it or not, according to statistics you can have up to thirty close friends. Now I think you need extremely sharp time management skills to handle that. You might also want to attend a workshop on stress management. Friendship takes work; it requires time and effort. Close, long-lasting friendships do not just happen. You can develop close relationships with people based on the activities you share with them: members of a club, an organization, or a church ministry. A person who gives input or provides guidance and direction in your life is a close friend.

Close friends always have something in common. The common goal for the mentoring relationship is the knowledge or skill being developed. For the associate friendship, it is the association, organization, or committee. So what are the common goals in your relationships? In every interpersonal relationship that a Christian has, Christ should be both the foundation and common goal. Either we are spending time with people who know the Lord, and He is our focus as we challenge one another to grow spiritually; or we are spending time with unsaved people, and the Lord is still our focus as we help them know the love of Jesus Christ.

We all have a hole in our soul that can only be filled with the love of Christ. Consequently, people who are unsaved have a deep hunger that needs to be filled. As Christians, we know that only the love of Jesus can fill that hole. And so our goal is always—even with our unsaved friends—to share and show the love of Christ. They are in need, and we have the answer. We are not the answer, but we do have the answer. We can direct them to the Lord Jesus Christ.

■ *Intimate Best Friends*

At the top level is the intimate best friend. Ideally, this is the kind of relationship that you want to share with your spouse. Unfortunately, there are not many married couples who can say that they are best friends. Some are good friends. Many are somewhat close, but not necessarily the best of friends. An intimate best friend is the person to whom you can tell your most cherished secrets. This person understands you. They will be there for you no matter what happens. This person understands your joys, your triumphs, and your sorrows. He is someone who is there to comfort you—who wants to be with you and spend time with you. This person is a whole person without you and you are whole without him. Otherwise, you will not achieve this level of friendship. Early in our marriage, neither José nor I was whole. I was pompous and he was lost! But what a joy it is when you come to yourself in Christ; then you and your spouse can share this type of intimacy.

Stop and evaluate your marital relationship; then evaluate yourself. What level would you say that you and your spouse are on? What level are you on with yourself? With God? Is your spouse more of an acquaintance or just a casual friend? Take time right now to pray. Ask the Lord to take your relationship to the next level, and know that He can take your marriage to the top.

A Friendship That Supersedes All Others

Our relationship with Christ is the most important relationship that we will ever have. He is our sufficiency. He is our salvation. He is our strength. If you looked at the diagram and thought that God would be your intimate best friend, remember that God is off the scale. Our relationship with the Lord supersedes yet permeates every other relationship. There is no way to classify Him or limit

Him to a particular level. God is everything. The Lord Jesus enables us to move from one level to the next in our relationships, so we must develop our relationship with Christ first. If we do not have an intimate relationship with the Lord, it is difficult to be in right relationship with anyone else. He must be the foundation.

Our vital spiritual relationship with the Lord also takes time and effort. We must cultivate this relationship. Jesus is waiting to spend time with each of us. He is waiting for us to slow down long enough to fit Him in. Too often, we get up and rush off into our day saying: "God knows my schedule." "I have five kids." "I have to get to work." "I have to do this and that." And we rush past the room where He is waiting. He is there with His arms outstretched saying, "I want to be your friend, too. Come and sit and sup with Me."

Are you spending the time and making the effort to know Him better through personal prayer and Bible study? Do not ignore the Lord or become too busy. Do not let your actions shout, "You will just have to wait." Make it your priority to spend time with Him.

Scripture says, "A man that hath friends must shew himself friendly: and there is a friend that sticketh closer than a brother" (Proverbs 18:24 KJV). Jesus desires to have a relationship with us that supersedes all others. He also wants to introduce us to the Father.

Jesus Christ is not only Lord of our lives; He is also our perfect example of a friend. The actions and principles of His life can help us discover how to be a friend, how to make friends, and how to determine our capacity for friendship.

Jesus had many acquaintances. He was acquainted with the masses and the world. However, when Christ came to earth, He did not hang out with all the people who were religious. Jesus spent time with the Pharisees, but His relationship with them was not a friendly one.

Jesus also had casual friends. The Bible talks about a crowd of people who followed Him as He went from town to town. Jesus' casual friends included men and women of substance (Matthew 27:55–56; Luke 8:2–3; 23:27, 49), the seventy disciples (Luke 10:1– 17), and the crowd of people who followed Him (Mark 3:9; Luke 8:45). Jesus saw these people on a regular basis.

Jesus had twelve close friends—the twelve apostles. When you consider how many times in the New Testament that we read about Jesus and the twelve apostles, it is evident that He spent a lot of time with them. So when we talk about having as many as thirty close friends, remember that the Lord Himself only had twelve.

Among these twelve, there were a few disciples with whom Jesus shared an even closer relationship. Do you know who Jesus' best friends were? (The answer is not the Father.)

Jesus' intimate best friends were Peter, James, and John. The Scriptures describe their relationship with Jesus. Matthew 17:1 says, "And after six days Jesus taketh Peter, James, and John his brother, and bringeth them up into a high mountain apart" (KJV). In Mark 5:37, it reads, "And he suffered no man to follow him, save Peter, and James, and John" (KJV). Peter, James, and John were with Jesus when He went to pray. They were with Him at the Mount of Transfiguration. Throughout the Gospels, we read how Jesus was traveling along with the twelve disciples, and then He took Peter, James, and John and pulled them aside (Mark 9:2; 13:3; 14:33; Luke 6:14; 8:51; 9:28). These three men were often separated for intimate conversation and instruction.

When you consider your very close friends, ask yourself who are the Peter, James, and John in your life. Who are the people or the person with whom you can share your challenges and triumphs? When you are rejoicing, whom can you count on to be happy with you? When you're going through difficulties, whom can you ask to stand or pray with you?

Finally, above every other relationship Jesus also had the ultimate Best Friend. Remember, there is a higher level. Jesus' relationship with God the Father superseded every human relationship (cf. Matthew 12:47–50; Luke 2:49). Jesus' desire was that we would become like Him and the Father. "The sheep that are My own hear and are listening to My voice; and I know them, and they follow Me. And I give them eternal life, and they shall never lose it or perish throughout the ages. [To all eternity they shall never by any means be destroyed.] And no one is able to snatch them out of My hand. My Father, Who has given them to Me, is greater and mightier than all [else]; and no one is able to snatch [them] out of the Father's hand. I and the Father are One" (John 10:27–30 AMPLIFIED).

That is Jesus' desire for us—that we will be one with Him as He is one with the Father. That is the most intimate relationship. That is as close as you can get.

THE BUILDING BLOCKS OF FRIENDSHIP

The diagram below illustrates the building blocks of friendship. Notice that the two pillars on the side are time and effort, and Jesus is the foundation.

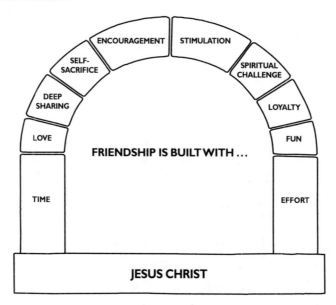

Figure 7-2

Friends and Friendship: The secrets of Drawing Closer by Jerry and Mary White. NavPress Singapore (exclusively available in the U.S. through Castle Bookstore, The Navigators, P.O. Box 6819, Colorado Springs, CO 80934, 719.272.7410, castlebookstore@navigators.com)

When you are building a friendship with your spouse, it takes: love, deep sharing, self-sacrifice, encouragement, mental stimulation, spiritual challenge, loyalty, and fun. What is your relationship missing? In which areas do you need to develop more?

Building with God's Love—When you talk about love as a building block for the relationship, it is love based on 1 Corinthians 13.

> First Corinthians 13:4–8a: *Love endures long and is patient and kind; love never is envious nor boils over with jealousy, is not boastful or vainglorious, does not display itself haughtily. It is not conceited (arrogant and inflated with pride); it is not rude (unmannerly) and does not act unbecomingly. Love (God's love in us) does not insist on its own rights or its own way, for it is not self-seeking; it is not touchy or fretful or resentful; it takes no account of the evil done to it [it pays no attention to a suffered wrong]. It does not rejoice at injustice and unrighteousness, but rejoices when right and truth prevail. Love bears up under anything and everything that comes, is ever ready to believe the best of every person, its hopes are fadeless under all circumstances, and it endures everything [without weakening]. Love never fails [never fades out or becomes obsolete or comes to an end]."* (AMPLIFIED)

Most people think, "I will give something to you if you give something to me." That attitude is part of the "give to get in return" syndrome. I recognize the distinction between my definition of love and God's love in me when I think about my husband's friends and how they always wanted to come over to our house. I was a Christian, but I was not demonstrating the love of Christ. When they came over, my first statement would be, "They have to go in the basement. They will be loud. I don't want to hear the profanity. They will want to drink." We don't have ashtrays in our house, so when they came over I always heard the question, "Man, where is the ashtray?" I would quickly respond, "On the porch. You cannot smoke in our house."

Now there is nothing wrong with telling people that they cannot smoke in your house because you do not want to smoke up the drapes and smell up the furniture, but you send another message when there is a bad attitude evident in the way you say it. It is the response that you give people. I had a very haughty attitude whenever I would tell them that they could not smoke in my house. "This is a God-fearing home, and we will not have that." I was my husband's good Christian wife. His friends were probably thinking, "Man, is that the way she acts all the time?" Of course in the meantime, my husband was telling everybody that he has this great wife, and she goes to church, and she counsels other Christian women, and she helps people with their problems. But when his friends came to our house, they thought, "Is this the woman you have been talking about?"

Now I thank God that my husband is a very strong man and that he loves me in spite of myself, because his friends could have deterred him. I was definitely not all that Christ would have me to be and I still am not, but I am growing. And even through all of that, my husband was willing to stay with me. Several years ago, I was out with some women sharing about my marriage and some of the difficult times and I said, ". . . you know, and I stayed with him." I heard myself speak and I thought, "Still full of pride, Sabrina. The Lord still has so much work to do on and in you. Not only did you stay with him; he stayed with you."

It takes two to build a marriage. And even as Christian women, we often are not "all good," and we are not always everything that we think we are. We have faults and do some things that probably drive our husbands crazy as well. However, we must remember that God's love never fails. Scripture says, "A friend loveth at all times, and a brother is born for adversity" (Proverbs 17:17 KJV). Knowing that a friend loves at all times is important because we know that everything is not always good. In difficult times, your acquaintances—all those people that you know—are nowhere to be found. But your friends are right there with you in the midst of what is going on. They may counsel, confront, and correct you, but they are there for you.

So remember that the love you want to show toward your spouse is based on 1 Corinthians 13. You also need to demonstrate the love of Christ to his friends.

Building with Deep Sharing—A friend is a person who should be able to counsel you regarding your situations in life, someone you should be able to turn to as it relates to your marriage. Not everyone can be this kind of friend. Too often when we hear people talk about deep sharing and friendships, they want to play "Twenty Questions." But the truth is: You really do not need to know all of someone's business to be his or her friend. Deep sharing involves being transparent and able to say what the Lord is doing in your life. I think that is the most important thing that we need to share. Not just how we feel, but also how God is responding to our feelings and our situations. "Is God telling me to wait? Is He telling me to forge ahead? Has He sent me into deep study and to a certain portion of Scripture, and I want to share some insights that I have gained?" That is the type of deep sharing we should do, something more on a spiritual level.

Building with Self-Sacrifice—In order to build relationships, we must make some sacrifices. You have to do some things that you would not normally do. God knows your heart. Keep in mind that it is the motivation of man that God is concerned with, not the outward appearance (1 Samuel 16:7).

When I was first saved, I jumped into the Christian life determined to go full speed ahead. Now, I would have never considered going to any of the places that my husband and I had been before. Not that there was anything wrong with those places, but that is what I did when I was unsaved. I thought, "Christians go to church. They go visit people at the hospital. They take cookies to the new neighbors. I cannot just go to the park; that is a waste of time, you know." So I developed this lifestyle that was almost anti-social. I started to limit myself, and I began to build a wall of just Christian people and just Christian activities.

However, as I learned about the importance of being a witness for God in my home, I realized that I had to become willing to go more places with my unsaved husband. So we went to a couple of sporting events. (I do not like sports, unfortunately.) There was baseball and basketball—I didn't even know all the names of the key players. I was even in a football pool, not because I like to gamble, nor because I wanted to make some money, but because it was an activity that I could do with my husband. There were other couples involved in the football pool, and it was something that I knew he liked. Was that something that I would normally do? Was it something that I cared about? No. But every week, we sat down at the table to laugh and talk about what happened. I even watched a few games so that we could talk about the players. My objective was to build our relationship and spend time with him.

Scripture teaches us, "For, brethren, ye have been called unto liberty; only use not liberty for an occasion to the flesh, but by love serve one another" (Galatians 5:13 KJV). Consider those areas or things in which you need to make some sacrifices.

Building with Encouragement—You need to learn how to encourage your spouse. Remember that we all have a hole in our soul that can only be filled with the love of Christ. Think about the various relationships that your spouse has: he/she has relationships at work, the people at the gym or wherever he/she goes for any type of recreational activities, his/her friends, etc. These are all relationships that are filling the voids in his/her life—satisfying his/her need for love and esteem. You want to be careful about what is put into that hole in your soul. Once so much has been put in, nothing else can get in. Make sure that you are helping to fill your spouse's need for love and encouragement. You can never become your spouse's sufficiency, but you can help to encourage and build your mate up. Scripture has called us to edify one another, and that is what you want to do for your mate. "Let us therefore follow after the things which make for peace, and things wherewith one may edify another" (Romans 14:19 KJV). "Wherefore comfort yourselves together, and edify one another, even as also ye do" (1 Thessalonians 5:11 KJV).

Encourage your spouse in every way possible. It should not be his secretary telling him how nice he looks, how intelligent he is, what a great idea he had, or how she appreciates the fact that he notices little things. That is the role of a wife. Whatever it is that you can think about to praise your husband and encourage him for, do that. You want to help build him up.

When I started to do this with my husband, I was amazed at his response. All of a sudden, he started to come to me just to talk about what was going on. He appreciated the encouragement and the feedback that I gave him on a regular basis. Initially, it was an exercise. I started doing it as a result of reading a book entitled *Building Your Mate's Self-Esteem* by Dennis and Barbara Rainey. My approach had always been: it may be a good book and I may try a few principles, but if there is no immediate change, I will just throw the book aside and keep moving. But when I saw some change I thought, "Wow, this really works," and I hung in there.

My husband says that he can always tell when I have read a new book or been to a seminar, because I come home with all of these great new ideas and techniques. So he has learned over the years to just bide the time and see what lasts. He admitted that what he had started to do was not to respond at all, just to see how long I would keep it up.

When I applied what I had learned but received no response from my husband, I would begin to get discouraged. But God started to convict me, and I began to realize that these were not just worldly techniques—much of it was biblical principle. God's Word will not return void. "So shall my word be that goeth forth out of my mouth: it shall not return unto me void, but it shall accomplish that which I please, and it shall prosper in the thing whereto I sent it" (Isaiah 55:11 KJV). God's Word is true. I can always stand on His Word regardless of the change I see. That is self-sacrifice. That is 1 Corinthians 13 love. Therefore, I had to ask myself, "Am I going to do it anyway?"

Persevere in encouraging your spouse and let everything that you do be done for Christ. Your spouse will benefit simply because you are obeying Christ. In other words, because you desire to please the Lord in your relationship with your husband, He will bless. Know that God is the One who can see change on the inside.

Hebrews 3:13 says that we are to "exhort one another daily, while it is called To day; lest any of you be hardened through the deceitfulness of sin" (KJV). I think that it is interesting that we are called to encourage one another daily. As you think about your marriage relationship and your friendships, ask yourself, "Have I encouraged my spouse or my friends today?" Remember that Scripture says we are to encourage others daily.

Too often, when we think about friendship, we are thinking about what someone else should do for us. But whenever we are looking for what someone will do for us, we need to look up. Only Christ can fill that void—whatever it is that we are looking for, whatever it is that we need. When we talk about friendship, we need to look at what we can do for someone else. What can we give to them? It should never become a situation where we think, "OK, I have encouraged you two times, but you have only encouraged me once." As a friend, I need to encourage you daily and I need to continue to encourage you.

You may think, "You know, I said some nice things to him yesterday." But continue to encourage your spouse. Some things that you do can really make a difference, even though you may not see it. So continue to encourage your spouse even if he/she never says anything about it. You have no idea what impact your encouragement may have. Be comforted knowing you are in God's will. The results rest with God.

Building with Stimulation—Stimulation involves more than just physical stimulation. There is mental stimulation. You need to be able to hold a conversation. I am not a "current events" person. In contrast, my husband is a history major. It seems he knows everything that has taken place during the course of the world. To have a conversation with my husband, I have to at least know what is going on in the world, because otherwise we will be talking about two totally different things. While I want to talk about all the current activities at the church, what I am planning to do, the locations of my speaking engagements, and what is happening with the bookstore or other business ventures, he wants to talk about world politics and sports.

In order to hold a conversation, we needed to enter each other's world. We do this by listening, asking questions, and encouraging our spouse to share with us. When mental stimulation is not provided at home, a married man or woman will often find it somewhere else.

Building with Spiritual Challenge—It is interesting that even while your spouse is unsaved, you can encourage him or her spiritually. I know that a lot of unsaved people are good people, but that does not make them God-fearing people. But it caused me to wonder, "What is God really doing in my husband's life?" When I stopped judging him, I could see him more as Christ saw him.

When I considered the number of spiritual activities my husband was engaged in, I knew that God was working in his life. Every now and then I would have a glimmer of hope and think, "Man, I wonder if he is saved and just waiting to tell me," because some days he was so kind. He was and is the most thoughtful man I have ever met. He is just a generous soul by nature. Therefore, as we spent time together,

I needed to be sure to encourage him spiritually—to challenge him spiritually. For example, when he talked about what was going on at the job and how he wanted to respond to certain things, I would ask him, "If God was there, would you still do that?" And he would say, "Well, God will understand." Then I would ask, "Would He really?" This often created an opportunity to talk about spiritual things.

I had learned from experience that ramming the Word down his throat is not a good approach to challenge your spouse spiritually. Scripture admonishes us: "And let us consider and give attentive, continuous care to watching over one another, studying how we may stir up (stimulate and incite) to love and helpful deeds and noble activities" (Hebrews 10:24 AMPLIFIED). Take time to consider how you can build your friendships and your relationship with your spouse by sensitively and appropriately using spiritual challenge and encouragement.

Building with Loyalty—As mentioned earlier, a loyal friend refuses to gossip. Be loyal to your husband; part of being loyal is not telling everybody else his faults. Giving your friends a list of your spouse's faults is not a good idea. Because when you have made up and you are all in love again and telling everybody how great he is, they will be ready to remind you of all the things that he has done to you, and they will be waiting to ask you, "How do you stay with him?" or "Why do you stay with him?" So do not give them his fault list.

Galatians 6:2 says, "Bear ye one another's burdens, and so fulfil the law of Christ" (KJV). It is interesting that Scripture specifically refers to bearing another's "burdens." In *Strong's Concordance* it says that a burden is really like a boulder; it is a heavy load that a person cannot bear by himself or herself at the time. They need someone to come alongside them to help them for a season. To find out how loyal a friend really is, ask yourself: Is this person willing to help me bear life's burdens?

Sometimes we have to ask ourselves if we are bearing another's burden or simply carrying their knapsack. There are many people who will ask you to carry their knapsack. It is like saying, "Well, I do not want to carry this today. Here, you carry it." Then you find yourself running around (being responsible) for everybody else. That is not really bearing one another's burdens.

We need to develop friendships with people who are loyal and learn to be a loyal friend ourselves. A loyal friend will give your knapsack back to you because you need to be responsible for it. But he or she will also help you to carry the burdens of life because there are times when life can become very heavy.

Building with Fun—Finally, friendship needs to be fun. Did you know that having fun is biblical? I have run across people who haven't laughed out loud in months. I just cannot imagine living without laughter. I laugh out loud at least once every day, even when I am by myself. I just get tickled by something and laughter will burst out. Scripture tells us that laughter is like good medicine (Proverbs 17:22a). We need to be healthy as we develop relationships with other people. So laugh a lot. We should not wait for people to bring laughter to us. We need to take laughter to them. Some people just need to lighten up a little. People often sing, "This is the day that the Lord has made. I will rejoice and be glad in it." When you are rejoicing and you are glad, when you are excited and happy, and when you are having fun or having a good time, you bless those around you. Your enthusiasm for the Lord can be contagious.

I am probably the most serious person I know. But nobody wants to be around a "stick in the mud." Every time they see you, it is "the weight of life." You need to lighten up, especially at home. By all means, lighten up and have some fun together with your spouse. Your husband/wife should not always see your serious, somber side. He or she should want to be with you because when you are together you have a good time; you both should have fun together.

Make this your prayer.

Dear Lord, Teach me to see my spouse as my most valued friend. May we grow in our friendship with each other until our intimacy incorporates body, soul, and spirit. Identify the areas of need in our lives that You have designed for us to meet only in each other. Help us to be transparent. Also, give me discernment regarding my friendships. Reveal those friendships that draw me closer to You and support my most valued friendship with my spouse. Help me to discern any relationships that are unhealthy for my marriage and to act accordingly. In Jesus' name. Amen.

Prayers
Jackie
Nate > *pastor* Mikes son in Guate
Courtney's safe travels to cincinati
Chris's son Jordan

Nancy to gym
& John got job

CHAPTER EIGHT

Giving Him Something He Can Feel

D o you remember a movie made in the '70s entitled *Sparkle?* In the movie, three sisters performed the song "Giving Him Something He Can Feel." The words are "I am giving him something he can feel to let him know my love is real." Remember that? Remember the movements? "I am giving him something he can feel (hands up and shake your hips) to let him know this love is real, this love is real." Now, that was a secular movie, but as I thought about it in this context, it has a biblical application.

God gave us something that we could feel. God so loved us that He gave His only begotten Son (John 3:16). He made a way for us to come unto Him when we were most unlovable. While we were yet sinners, while we were in our mess, God loved us and Christ gave His life for us (Romans 5:8).

Just as the Lord gave, we also should give. Yet we, who have received the awesome love of God that forgave us our sins, too often judge our husbands. We say, "I am going to love him when he deserves it." And while we wait for him to earn our love, we are foolishly tearing down our marriage with our own hands (cf. Proverbs 14:1).

Just as you will build your friendship with your husband, build your home with the love of God. Give your husband something he can feel in the following areas.

GIVE HIM SOMETHING PHYSICAL AND SOMETHING SPIRITUAL

Your husband has feelings too, and he really does want you to give him something he can feel. Now when you give your husband something he can feel, you need to give him something physical and something spiritual. You both can share the love of God and the physical love that God has intended for marriage.

First Corinthians 3:16 asks the question, "Know ye not that ye are the temple of God, and that the Spirit of God dwelleth in you?" (KJV). If we truly believed that we had the Spirit of God living on the inside of us, we would begin to understand that we usher in the very presence of God everywhere we go—even in bed! This is only true if you know Him; if you know the One who is the Lover of your soul. If you feel loved because you have been spending time with God, then you will have something to give. You need to have and feel the love of God in your own life in order to give it. If you possess it, then you can share it. If you have not been spending time with the Lord, you will not want to be bothered with people, let alone love somebody, or make love to anybody.

As a professional counselor, I am in a practice called the Abundant Life Counseling Center, and it is my goal to help God's people live the abundant life. The "abundant life," for me, includes abundance in marriage. So, I encourage my clients to want and expect more. "Why just have sex when you can have maximum sex—when you can make love?" There is a difference between having sex and making love. When you make love, your husband should feel the love of God flowing from you. It really ought to be that good. I mean,

"Mmmm, gooood." You ought to say that, and your husband ought to say that because he can feel the love of God.

It will not be maximum sex if you just go through the motions or do your duty because Scripture says you have to. And Scripture *does* say you should do it. I know some women are probably familiar with this passage of Scripture and do not like it, but the Word of God is still true. First Corinthians 7:3–5 says, "The husband should fulfill his marital duty to his wife, and likewise the wife to her husband. The wife's body does not belong to her alone but also to her husband. In the same way, the husband's body does not belong to him alone but also to his wife. Do not deprive each other except by mutual consent and for a time, so that you may devote yourself to prayer. Then come together again so that Satan will not tempt you because of your lack of self-control" (NIV).

I find it interesting that Scripture tells us right up front that we lack self-control. As Christians, we wonder why premarital and extramarital sexual activity run rampant in our society. Scripture clearly says we lack self-control. Yet, many of us continue to deprive our spouse of what they need, and we know that they lack self-control. The question you must ask yourself is: "Am I really serious about building my marriage?" If you are serious, then you will not deprive your spouse.

GIVE HIM A GOOD ATTITUDE

I have decided and determined that I am serious about this thing called marriage. I am serious about loving my husband. I am serious about making him feel good. I am serious about his knowing how much I love God and his understanding the fact that my love for God is making a difference for him. I am serious about this thing. And when I make love with José, he knows that he has been in the presence of God. How does he know? Because I bring the love of God and my love for him with me every time we come together.

In one situation a couple came in for counseling. The woman was so furious with her husband that she demanded that they get marriage counseling; she had an attitude that you would not believe. I could hear it in her tone of voice as she said, "I have tried having sex with him. I have even tried to approach him. He had the audacity to roll over and kiss me and say, 'Honey, thank you, but no. I do not want to trouble you.'"

I turned to him and asked, "Why was that trouble?" And he said, "Let me tell you my side. For the last three months, every time I have approached her, it has been trouble. On at least thirty-seven occasions she had such a bad attitude, I didn't want to be close to her. On some nights it was just too hot for her; other nights it was too cold. Some nights it was too early; then it was too late. Other nights she did not want to awaken the baby, or she was afraid the kids were going to hear us. Some nights she had not taken a bath yet; other nights she did not want to get herself dirty because she had just taken a bath." He said, "It was just too much trouble for her. So I did not want to trouble her."

Then I asked his wife, "Now let me make sure I understand. You brought him in for counseling because you are angry with him? And you are upset because he kissed you and said, 'Thank you, but no'?" Who could blame him? He didn't want to trouble her.

Lest we ignore her "issues," her complaints were real ones. Many women have voiced these same concerns when it comes to making love. Environmental factors cannot be overlooked. However, that is where effective communication comes in (see chapter 6). Her concerns were legitimate, but so were his.

And unfortunately, that is the very same attitude that many of us give our husbands: "It's too much trouble; I don't want to be bothered. Do you have any idea of the day that I've had? All of the things that I've had to do? All of the responsibilities that I have to carry out?" However, Scripture tells us your body does not even belong to you. Do not deprive your husband. Having sex with your husband

—making love to your husband—is a ministry that is reciprocal.

GIVE HIM SEXUAL FULFILLMENT

One of the things that I realize as I make love to my husband is that it is a prime opportunity to pray for him. I get to lay my hands all over him and bless every part of his body from the top of his head to the soles of his feet. I rub him down with oil and I pray, "Lord, bless him and keep him. Let him desire the wife of his youth." I want him to want me. I spend that time as necessary. I do not deprive him. When I am most tired, that is when I realize I need to die to self. I need to beat my body into subjection. I need to make my flesh do right, because my body is not my own. It belongs to him; it is rightly his.

I think that we require a lot of our men. We say, "Marry me first." That is wonderful; that is biblical. But when we say: "Marry me and keep yourself only unto me; I'm only going to want you half of the time, but keep yourself only unto me. I'm only going to want to make love to you when it's convenient, but keep yourself only unto me," we are requiring a lot. With conditions, we say, "Keep yourself only unto me," but Scripture says do not deprive him, otherwise he is going to be tempted because he lacks self-control.

I know that some of you probably cannot relate to this. Maybe you do not deprive your husbands of anything. You are very submissive and loving, you are kind and generous, and you are always giving. But there are others who need to heed the following directive from the Lord: Go home and bless the brother! That is straight from the Lord. I was trying to sleep one night before a speaking engagement, and at three o'clock the Lord said, "Women need to go home and bless the brother." That is all there is to it.

GIVE HIM DOMESTIC SUPPORT

Get back to basics. Some husbands would feel blessed if their wives would just go home and clean the house. There is a book out by Dr. Glenn Zaepfel entitled *He Wins, She Wins*. In it, he describes the basic needs of men. One of the needs a man has is for domestic support, which means keeping your house clean. Simply do what you are supposed to do around the house (or pay someone else), and don't complain about what you are doing. Similarly, your husband needs to have a job; he needs to be able to provide for you. When he provides for you, whether you have a little house or a big house, you need to keep it clean.

Some of you are thinking, "Well, you know, if I had more space, I could keep it clean. There's just too much stuff." Well, throw out some of that clutter. Why are you keeping all of that old stuff? Get rid of it. Be a blessing to your husband by providing a clean environment. Can you imagine the difference in his attitude when he comes in and finds that everything is in order? Try it and see what a difference it would make.

Scripture tells us that the husband should be able to provide for his wife. "But if any provide not for his own, and specially for those of his own house, he hath denied the faith, and is worse than an infidel" (1 Timothy 5:8 KJV). Before God gave Eve to Adam, He gave him a job. First God gave him work to do, and then He gave him a helpmate. "And the Lord God took the man, and put him into the garden of Eden to dress it and to keep it" (Genesis 2:15 KJV). I realize that in our modern society this concept of home life is outmoded. Women are in corporate America and some men are "Mr. Moms." So do what works for your household. The idea here is that you each support your household in a way that shows the love of Christ.

GIVE HIM A PLAYMATE

In counseling, a wife's most common complaints about her husband are: "He doesn't love me," "He won't talk to me," or "He will not communicate with me." However, men are not necessarily looking for communication. Men are looking for someone to do activities with; they are looking for a playmate.

Very often, women do not want to go out and play. "I don't like sports. I don't like watching football. I don't want to see basketball. I'm not interested in golf. I don't want to go kayaking. I don't want to go rock climbing. I don't want to do any of that macho guy stuff." But your husband is looking for a playmate; if he is not playing with you, he is going to be playing with someone.

Anne shared how Miguel's primary sports interest is football and how she could not bring herself to watch a game with him. One Sunday, the game was on and she happened to respond to a touchdown play. He looked at her and smiled. He didn't say anything then, but a few days later he commented, "I just wanted you to know that I was happy to see that you could enjoy a game with me."

Changing your perspective on some things will help. You are supposed to be a suitable helpmate for your husband. So help him relax; help him enjoy; help him have fun. You must be careful not to become one of those saved women (like I was) who are so holy that they forget about living. They just can't do anything anymore, and they don't want their husbands to do anything either. Don't use the excuse I did: "Well, I don't like his friends." I learned that I shouldn't avoid associating with my husband's friends. In fact, I try to be with every one of his friends, especially those I don't like, so that I can be praying for them. That way I can know their character, I can know what my husband has been exposed to, I can try to see what he sees, and I can know what kind of influence they might have. I want to know those people; I don't want to just send him off with them. I want to go with him so that I can see what is going on, so that I will know how to pray for them. I have also learned that I don't need to watch my husband. I trust God to keep him, but I need to be wise in what I do. Remember that your husband is looking for a playmate, and you are his preference.

GIVE HIM A WARM RECEPTION

How many times have you said, "Well, what am I supposed to do with the kids? You know we can't get a sitter," "I have too much work to do," or "I'm tired"? You will always have excuses. There are always good reasons to put your husband off. You are not the first woman to do that. In fact, women all over the world are doing that. That is what keeps prostitutes in business. It is what keeps the adulterous women busy. Every time you say, "Scat, cat," there is some other woman saying, "Here, kitty, kitty, kitty. Here, kitty, kitty, kitty." You are sending him away, and he is looking for something to do. But he'd rather be doing it with you. Next time he wants to go somewhere, try saying, "Yes, honey, what time should I be ready?"

The Song of Solomon tells the story of a woman who sent her lover away. In the beginning of the book, they are calling each other by love names. He refers to her as his beloved, and she calls him her lover. They describe the beauty they see in each other, talk about how great the other is, and share all the things they desire to do together.

However, when we get to chapter 5 and verse 2, the woman says: "I slept but my heart was awake. Listen! My lover is knocking." He calls out to her: "Open to me, my sister, my darling, my dove, my flawless one. My head is drenched with dew, my hair with the dampness of the night." Her response in verses 3–6: "I have taken off my robe—must I put it on again? I have washed my feet—must I soil them again? My lover thrust his hand through the latch-opening; my heart began to pound for him. I arose to open for my lover, my hands dripped with myrrh, my fingers with flowing myrrh, and on the handles of the lock. I opened for my lover, but my lover had left; he was gone. My heart sank at his departure. I looked for him but did not find him. I called him but he did not answer" (NIV).

Now, it is interesting that in the beginning of the book, they are constantly making love with each other. But in chapter 5, she says, "You know what? I am just tired." In those days, they locked the door with a big heavy latch so you could not open it with a key from the outside. The bridal chamber was part of the inner court. In order to answer the door, the woman had to literally get up out of the bridal bed, go down to the door, and take the heavy latch off to let someone in. When her lover came knocking on the door in the middle of the night, she lies there thinking, "I am in the bed. I have taken off my robe. I have bathed my body. Now you want me to get my feet dirty walking across the room to open the door to let you in?"

Finally, she says to herself, "What is wrong with me? Let me get up and go let in my lover." But when she gets to the door, he is gone. She says, "I looked for him, and I could not find him." She goes out into the night looking around trying to find him, asking, "Have you seen him? Have you seen him?" (v. 6).

Similarly, some of your husbands are out in the street, and you are wondering, "Has anybody seen him?" You have sent him away. You were too busy or too tired. It was too cold or too hot. You were too clean, or you were too dirty. You had a headache. It was that time of the month. It was the kids. It was always something. You sent him away, and now he is out in the street.

GIVING HIM THE RIGHT ATMOSPHERE

In Proverbs chapter 7, the adulterous woman talks about how she lures men in. The passage describes exactly what she does in detail. It says that she sets her house in order; her house is clean. She does not have stacks of books lying on the floor; she does not have work from the office sitting on the nightstand. Not only is her house clean, but she has scented her bed chamber with oil. She has created an environment that says, "Come, let me love you." Her bedroom is a place to make love, and she lures men there. The adulterous woman has gotten herself together, she has gotten her house in order, and she is waiting, while we send our husbands out into the streets.

Unfortunately, 63 percent of all marriages end in divorce. Most divorces occur as the result of adultery. Some of you have lived through adultery, and your marriage has survived. Some of you are dealing with it now but don't know it. Others have lived through it and are barely making it. Too often, women see adultery as an out— a reason for divorce. Yes, adultery was given in Scripture as grounds for divorce, but it was because of the hardness of men's hearts. "He saith unto them, Moses because of the hardness of your hearts suffered you to put away your wives: but from the beginning it was not so" (Matthew 19:8 KJV). In contrast, it is the Lord's desire that one would repent and the other would forgive. And as we forgive our husbands, then we need to learn how to love them. We also need to change the way we do things.

Let me be clear about this point: I am not at all implying that if a man has an adulterous affair that it is his wife's fault. Every man and every woman will indeed give an account to God for every deed that they have done. "So then every one of us shall give account of himself to God" (Romans 14:12 KJV). You can be the worst wife in the world and that is still no justification for your husband to have an affair. However, many of the things that we do can set up that type of situation. We deprive our husbands of sexual intimacy. We do not spend time with them. We do not meet their needs. So they go looking for a playmate or a playgirl.

GIVE HIM A CHEERLEADER

According to the book *His Needs, Her Needs* by Harley Willard Jr., a man wants a cheerleader. Can you imagine having the ongoing support of a cheerleader, someone who is rah, rah, rah, right there in your corner and enthusiastic about everything you do? When things are going well, they cheer you on with "Go, go, go." And when things are looking dim, they cheer "Defense" or "Hold that line."

What was the last thing that you praised your husband for? What was his last great accomplishment? Do you even know? Do you know what his dreams are? What his hopes are? What his desires are? Do you know what his struggles are? Do you know the things that concern him or the things that worry him? Are you right there encouraging him, speaking words of comfort to him? Are you holding his hand and praying with him about those things, or are you too busy to even notice? Are you a cheerleader for your husband?

Recently my husband came home with a golf trophy. He played in a tournament with the church league. All season long he had been talking about how bad his game was this year, how he was off, and how his score was too high for most of the game. He kept saying, "But, the one thing I can say is that I was honest. I was honest the whole game." The next time he played, I said, "Well, honey, how do you think you did?" And he said, "I am sure I did not do that well." And I said, "OK, but at least you were honest." He felt good about the fact that he was honest.

The season was almost fourteen weeks long, and every week he'd come home saying, "I didn't do that well, but I was honest about it. You see guys out there—it is hard to believe the guys are Christians; they are lying about their scores so they'll look good. But I was honest."

Then he came home from the banquet one day and put a trophy down on the table. He just smiled a little wry smile. I put everything down and jumped up and got excited. I could have looked at it and said, "Oh, that's nice," and kept right on typing on my computer. But I knew how important that trophy was to him because all season long he kept saying, "My game was off. I haven't done well. But at least I was honest." I looked at the trophy and I said, "You know what? The Lord has rewarded you. You were honest. Think about it; you have a trophy for third place with an honest score. That is better than being in first place and cheating. You had an honest score in third place." Then I asked him if he wanted to go out and celebrate.

It really was not that big of a deal to me, but it was important to him. And I knew how important that was to him. I don't want somebody else shouting and getting excited about what my husband does. I want to be the one who is excited about it. Third place is great because he was honest. In that situation, I also had an opportunity to praise the godly character I saw in him—the traits of honesty, diligence, faithfulness, and perseverance. Those are important qualities, and I am glad that he has those qualities.

Unfortunately, most of us don't listen enough to know what is important. Your beauty is going to fade, ladies. You will not always have your looks. But, attentiveness goes far beyond looks, far beyond physical beauty. Attention is alluring; men like women who pay them attention. People fall in love with the way you make them feel. They can literally love how you make them feel. Think about the people with whom you spend time. Usually, you spend time with them because they make you feel good. They make you laugh. They give you something to think about. They challenge you. You feel good when you are around them.

That is how your husband should feel about you. You should be his best friend. When he has something exciting to share, he should want to run home and tell you. He should want to call you and talk it over with you, because you are his best friend. Can you say that about your husband—that you are your husband's best friend? Maybe, maybe not. Some of you don't even know, because you have not spent enough time with the man God has given you to find out.

Give him something he can feel. Take the time to encourage him, to listen to him, to be happy for him.

GIVE HIM LOVE WHEN HE IS UNLOVABLE

When I was first saved, I was certain that my husband would be overjoyed. I was certain he would be so excited that I had found this new love in Jesus Christ. But it did not work that way. However, my husband's resentment did cause me to draw even closer to God. It strengthened me for the long haul. Now when something happens, I fall on my knees and say, "Lord, what would You have me to do? What do I need to do?" Too often, we point the finger at our spouses and say what he or she needs to do. But as Christians, we must do what is right, even when we are the only ones in the relationship willing to do it.

Scripture tells us not to grow weary in well-doing. "And let us not be weary in well doing: for in due season we shall reap, if we faint not" (Galatians 6:9 KJV). If one person in the household is living right, that house is still blessed. You can still make a difference. So what if you are the only one doing right? Remember that God will hold him accountable for what he is and is not doing. But if you try to render evil for evil or do what he does, God is going to judge you as well.

When Christians come in and say, "Well, he is not doing right. Why do I have to do right?" I just look at them and say, "Let the Spirit answer that for you." You have to live right because the Spirit of God is living in you. If the power of God is active and available in you and you really are utilizing that power, then living godly is possible. Blessing the brother and giving him something he can feel becomes easier because what he needs to feel most is the love of God.

Scripture says when we love those who are lovable, we really have not done anything. Non-Christians love those who are lovable. However, it is when we love those who are unlovable that we most resemble Christ.

> Luke 6:31–36: *And as ye would that men should do to you, do ye also to them likewise. For if ye love them which love you, what thank have ye? for sinners also love those that love them. And if ye do good to them which do good to you, what thank have ye? for sinners also do even the same. And if ye lend to them of whom ye hope to receive, what thank have ye? for sinners also lend to sinners, to receive as much again. But love ye your enemies, and do good, and lend, hoping for nothing again; and your reward shall be great, and ye shall be the children of the Highest: for he is kind unto the unthankful and to the evil. Be ye therefore merciful, as your Father also is merciful.* (KJV)

Remember, when we were most unlovable, that is when God gave His Son. When your husband is most unlovable, that is when he needs you the most. That is when you need to grab him and embrace him; you need to hold him and pray for him. If you are going to give him something he can feel, give him what he really needs to feel—the love of God flowing from you. As you give him something he can feel, it needs to go beyond just the physical; it must include the spiritual as well.

GIVE HIM A PRAYING WIFE

Scripture tells us that "charm is deceitful and beauty is fading, but a woman who fears the Lord will be praised" (Proverbs 31:30 paraphrased). That is the woman that a husband will love long-term. Your Dolly Parton breasts and your Tina Turner legs are not going to last forever. When your physical body starts to droop and sag, what will you have left? The godly women in the Bible adorned themselves in the beauty of the Lord by being in God's presence and by getting in His Word.

> First Peter 3:3–5: *Whose adorning let it not be that outward adorning of plaiting the hair, and of wearing of gold, or of putting on of apparel; But let it be the hidden man of the heart, in that which is not corruptible, even the ornament of a meek and quiet spirit, which is in the sight of God of great price. For after this manner in the old time the holy women also, who trusted in God, adorned themselves, being in subjection unto their own husbands.* (KJV)

If you really want to bless your husband, you need to become a mighty woman of God, a woman who knows how to pray about all things.

There is a book out by Stormie Omartian, *The Power of a Praying Wife*. In this book, she prays for her husband in thirty different areas of life. She prays about everything: his friends, his finances, his job, his attitude, his fathering, his role as husband. She covers everything. Where she starts, though, is by praying for herself: "Lord, help me to want to pray for him. Help me with my attitude. Help me to love him the way You love me."

GIVE HIM A WIFE WITH RIGHT PRIORITIES

The Lord has brought me alongside my husband as a suitable helpmate. I know that I can meet his needs. I am also very much aware that there is a deep longing in his soul that only the Lord can satisfy. I do not try to go there. But I do those things that the Lord has called me to do. I give him something that he can feel. My husband doesn't have to wonder if I love him. And it's not because I say, "Honey, I love you." I tell him that, but I also show him that. Love is action. Love is demonstrated in the simplest of things.

One way that you can demonstrate your love for your husband

is by having right priorities. God-given priorities are that:

1. God should be first.
2. Your spouse should be next.
3. Your children come after your spouse.
4. Your job, work, or vocation come behind the children.
5. Then your ministry is next.

Many women have their priorities totally out of order. They confuse ministry, which is priority number five, with God, who is number one. They confuse busyness and church work with holiness. Believe me, I know.

I can recall a time when I would come home from church and my husband would say, "If I want anything done around here, all I need to do is call the church and let your pastor tell you because you do what the pastor says to do. When the pastor says he needs somebody, you come running. When the pastor says there is a committee or a project, you show up. If I ask you to do something, you are too busy. So, if I want anything done, all I need to do is call the church."

Remember that serving on church committees doesn't make you more spiritual. It's easy to be at the church where everybody is praising God, shouting, singing, and dancing. It is easier to be in the company of other women than it is to be at home dealing with your husband. Like me, some of you need to go home and minister to your mate and family. You are involved in far too many ministries. I know it takes laborers in the vineyard to do the work of the ministry, but not every open position is for you to fill. You need to minister in your home. I know there are issues at home that many women are avoiding.

If your house is falling apart, your service at church is hypocrisy. You need to be giving what you have to the man God has given you. If there is any left, give to the church. Do not confuse your Christian service with your relationship with God. Your relationship with God is of paramount importance; that is indeed number one. But all of that service, all of that busyness, does not equate to relationship. If you really knew God the way some of you claim to know Him, you would also know how important your witness is to your spouse and how important your husband is to God. God wants you to love him; He wants you to demonstrate the love of God to him.

In another counseling situation, a pastor's wife had a major problem with the church secretary because the secretary knew the pastor so well. She knew what he liked and what he wanted. She knew his desires, hopes, dreams, and aspirations for the church and for his ministry. And she was right there supporting him and helping him meet every last one of them. The pastor's wife was certain that something was going on. However, according to the pastor—and I believe him—nothing inappropriate had taken place. But his wife felt threatened (and maybe guilty too) because another woman was meeting the same personal needs of her husband that she was not fulfilling. So, I challenged the pastor's wife, "You can blame her, or you can do something about it. What are you going to do about it?"

Each of you has an opportunity to do something. Stay home sometime and bless your husband. What are you so mad about? What are you so angry about? What are you holding on to that prevents you from blessing him? You need to bless the brother.

GIVE HIM A SWEET RESPONSE

Women usually have something to say. And some women seem to have a reply for everything. No matter what their husband says, they have something to say. However, if you would really stop and think before you speak, you would say less. As you give him something he can feel, you should not only watch what you say, but

CAN TWO WALK TOGETHER?

you should ask yourself whether some things should really be said at all.

In addition, you need to check the tone of voice you use when you speak. There are certain things I want to say, but I know that the way I would say it, even though there was no malice intended in my heart that I know about, would cause it to come out the wrong way. I can say this with assurance because Scripture says that our hearts are deceitful and wicked (Jeremiah 17:9) and that it is out of the issues of the heart that the mouth speaks (Luke 6:45). So if you are surprised by what you say or the tone in which you say it, don't think, "I don't know where that came from." It was in you; that's where it came from. If you sit around the house murmuring and complaining about all of the things that he is not and about all of the things he should be doing, eventually, given opportunity, those are the things that will come out of your mouth.

You also need to ask yourself if this is the right time to say it. There is a right time to say things. And if something must be said, the best time is after you have prayed about it. Before I say some of the things I want to say, I pray about it. Often, by the time I am done praying, I have missed the moment, and then I realize that it was not the right time to say it anyway. That is why it is so important to pray—to pray for him and to pray for yourself. "Lord, give me words to say that will be edifying, words that will build him up and not tear him down. I don't want to be guilty of tearing my house down with my own hands. Lord, help me to build him up." When I am praying and I miss the moment, I thank God I didn't say what was on my mind, because it would have been the wrong thing. Then I would have to spend weeks trying to make it right again.

When I am in a better frame of mind or at a better time, the Lord gives me exactly what to say. Sometimes it is just, "Yes, honey." When I say, "Yes, honey," I am being supportive. I often give this challenge as a homework assignment for women who struggle with submission: In response to whatever your husband says for the next week, just say, "Yes, honey," and then do it. Now, I give this same challenge to each of you reading this chapter: Starting today, as a sweet response to your husband, just say, "Yes, honey." When he says, "When you go downstairs, could you get me this?" say, "Yes, honey," and go and get it right then. Don't wait until it is convenient for you to go.

I remember a time when my husband said, "Sabrina, when you go downstairs, bring me a glass of Kool-Aid." I answered, "OK." And I kept right on doing what I was doing. He asked me again, "Are you going to get that Kool-Aid for me?" I said, "Yeah, you asked me to bring it when I go down. I haven't gone yet." I interpreted his request as, "Please do this whenever you go." But he was saying, "I am thirsty. Could you get me a drink?"

Now, if I run downstairs and get the Kool-Aid and say, "Here," I might as well throw it in his face. That is not, "Yes, honey." That is not a spirit of respect; it would not be done with love. If we give him something he can feel, make sure it is the right thing.

Bless your husband with a sweet response as often as you can, even if it is to make a request as simple as, "Go down and get me a drink." Just say, "Yes, honey," get up, and do whatever it is he has asked you to do. When he says, "Honey, would you put the kids to bed now? And could you keep them quiet?" answer "Yes, honey." Your sweet response to whatever he asks for during the next seven days will be something that he will feel. He will feel your support; he will feel your encouragement. That will bless the brother. Just hearing you say, "Yes, honey. Out of my respect for you, out of my love for you, I want to do these things for you."

Many of you have planted some bad seeds, and you are wondering about the stuff that is coming up. You do not plant and harvest in the same season. A lot of those things you have already planted are starting to come back and haunt you. You are wondering why your husband does not respond the way you want him to respond, and you have been loving him for the last two days. Well, you have been ugly for the last twelve. You have planted a lot of bad stuff. You have to go through and weed and clean out a lot of that and start to plant some new things. But for a while, the wheat is going to come up with the tares. Remember that you will eventually reap a harvest as you start now to plant loving seeds that your husband can respond to.

Give him something he can feel. Think about it. Everything you do causes your husband to feel something. Every action causes him to feel something. If you are aware of that, you'll be careful how you live. Scripture tells us to be careful how we live because the days are evil. "See then that ye walk circumspectly, not as fools, but as wise, redeeming the time, because the days are evil. Wherefore be ye not unwise, but understanding what the will of the Lord is" (Ephesians 5:15–17 KJV). We live in difficult times, and there is a lot of temptation in the world. So continue to pray for his strength and build him up as much as possible. Do not send him to the world to have his needs met. You have the opportunity to create an atmosphere in your home that will make it the best place in the world to be. Cultivate your relationship. Pray that he will experience so much of God by being with you that he would not want to be anyplace else.

Bless the brother, and take advantage of this prime opportunity to love him.

Let's pray.

Dear Lord, I thank You that You know what Your women need. You know what is best. Lord, I pray for the women who are reading this, for their homes, and for their husbands. I pray that they would be wise women, women who will build their households and not tear them down with their own hands. Help them not to deprive their husbands and send them out into the streets to the adulterous women. Father, help them to build their husbands up and bless them. Help them to give them something that they can feel: the love of God. In Jesus' name. Amen.

Moody Press, a ministry of Moody Bible Institute,
is designed for education, evangelization, and edification.
If we may assist you in knowing more about Christ
and the Christian life, please write us without obligation:
Moody Press, c/o MLM, Chicago, Illinois 60610.